A GIFT FOR

....

FROM

....

DATE

....

GOD'S LOVE
FOR
TODAY

GOD'S LOVE FOR TODAY

100 DEVOTIONS TO DRAW YOU CLOSER TO GOD

JACK COUNTRYMAN

God's Love for Today

© 2025 Jack Countryman

All rights reserved. No portion of this book may be reproduced, stored in a retrieval system, or transmitted in any form or by any means—electronic, mechanical, photocopy, recording, scanning, or other—except for brief quotations in critical reviews or articles, without the prior written permission of the publisher.

Published in Nashville, Tennessee, by Thomas Nelson. Thomas Nelson is a registered trademark of HarperCollins Christian Publishing, Inc.

Thomas Nelson titles may be purchased in bulk for educational, business, fundraising, or sales promotional use. For information, please email SpecialMarkets@ThomasNelson.com.

Unless otherwise noted, Scripture quotations are from the New King James Version®. Copyright © 1982 by Thomas Nelson. Used by permission. All rights reserved.

Scripture quotations marked NLT are from the Holy Bible, New Living Translation. Copyright © 1996, 2004, 2015 by Tyndale House Foundation. Used by permission of Tyndale House Ministries, Carol Stream, Illinois 60188. All rights reserved.

Any internet addresses, phone numbers, or company or product information printed in this book are offered as a resource and are not intended in any way to be or to imply an endorsement by Thomas Nelson, nor does Thomas Nelson vouch for the existence, content, or services of these sites, phone numbers, companies, or products beyond the life of this book.

Cover Design by Studio Gearbox
Interior Design by Kristy Edwards

ISBN 978-1-4002-4854-4 (HC)
ISBN 978-1-4002-4856-8 (audiobook)
ISBN 978-1-4002-4855-1 (eBook)

Printed in Malaysia

25 26 27 28 29 COS 10 9 8 7 6 5 4 3 2 1

Behold what manner of love the Father has bestowed on us, that we should be called children of God!

1 JOHN 3:1

CONTENTS

Introduction xiv

1: Called and Empowered to Love 2
2: Loving Much 4
3: Just as God Said 6
4: God's Law: A Gift of Love 8
5: Responding to God's Love 10
6: Walking with Our God 12
7: Walking in the Footsteps of Christ 14
8: Known by God 16
9: Loving Instruction 18
10: God's Broken Heart 20
11: Talking to the God Who Loves Us 22
12: Jesus' Sacrificial Love 24
13: Whosoever Believes 26
14: Four Heaven-Sent Gifts 28

15:	God's Merciful and Gracious Reach	30
16:	Loving Our Deliverer	32
17:	God's Open Arms	34
18:	Our Faithful, Loving God	36
19:	Our Rock, Fortress, and Deliverer	38
20:	Ambassadors and Advertisements	40
21:	Trust, Faith, and Joy	42
22:	It's All Faith	44
23:	Our Great God	46
24:	Chosen to Shine	48
25:	Walking in God's Righteousness	50
26:	Fight the Good Fight	52
27:	Living by Faith	54
28:	With All Our Hearts	56
29:	No Worries!	58
30:	The Lord Sees, Hears, Responds, and Comforts	60
31:	Promises of God	62
32:	Praise the Lord!	64
33:	A Proverb Is a Proverb	66
34:	The Gift of God's Wisdom	68
35:	Wisdom's Words	70
36:	God's Love Letter	72
37:	The Ultimate Act of Love	74
38:	Humbled and Able to Receive Wisdom	76
39:	Wise Counsel	78

40:	The Gift of God's Spirit	80
41:	What God Are You Following?	82
42:	Love Wisdom	84
43:	Love Your Enemies	86
44:	Where Your Treasure Is	88
45:	Will You Choose Life?	90
46:	Love Beyond Description	92
47:	Be at Peace	94
48:	The Blessings of Trusting God	96
49:	Greater Than We Can Imagine	98
50:	Joy in God's Word	100
51:	The Gift of God's Word	102
52:	Loving God's Testimonies	104
53:	No Longer Lukewarm	106
54:	Loving God and His Law	108
55:	The Inspired Word of God	110
56:	Seek What Is Good	112
57:	A Commendation	114
58:	Thirsting for the Lord	116
59:	A Labor of Love	118
60:	Imitating Christ	120
61:	An Appeal	122
62:	Prayer: A Language of Love	124
63:	Keep on Keeping On!	126
64:	Love Rooted in Faith in Christ	128

65:	Love Begets Growth—and More Love	130
66:	Humble Love	132
67:	Love That Acts	134
68:	Love Your Neighbor	136
69:	Doers of the Word	138
70:	God Loves All	140
71:	Words of Blessing	142
72:	Fruit of the Spirit	144
73:	Rejoicing in the Lord	146
74:	Whitewashed Tombs	148
75:	Darkness or Light?	150
76:	Resurrection Majesty and Power	152
77:	Hard Truth	154
78:	What God Has Planned for His People	156
79:	Our God Reigns	158
80:	A Love That Prays and Refreshes	160
81:	A Restored Relationship	162
82:	Seeing Our Sin	164
83:	Who Can Be Against Us?	166
84:	God's Ever-Present Love	168
85:	"I Am the Lord Your God"	170
86:	A Generous Eye	172
87:	A Soft Answer	174
88:	Always in My Prayers	176
89:	Love: A Paradigm Shifter	178

90:	Our Helper, Happiness, and Hope	180
91:	Faith in Times of Trouble	182
92:	The Love of a Jealous God	184
93:	The Goodness of the Lord	186
94:	God's 24/7 Goodness and Love	188
95:	Who Prays for You?	190
96:	When You Walk Through the Fire	192
97:	"See the Salvation of the LORD"	194
98:	Finding Strength for Today	196
99:	God's Grace and Mercy	198
100:	Responding with Love	200

Notes 203

About the Author 205

INTRODUCTION

When I started exploring the Bible on the subject of God's love, I discovered that the word *love* is found 504 times and the phrase *love of God* is mentioned sixty-eight times, which speaks volumes to the importance of God's love. The apostle John said that God is love (1 John 4:8), so it's no surprise love plays such a prominent role in Scripture. We can see throughout the Bible that our relationship with God is hinged not only on loving and worshiping Him but also on expressing love toward our fellow humans. Each page is a testament to God's yearning for us to realize and reflect His love.

Many of us live by the seat of our pants and often forget that God wants us to lean on Him for guidance in how we live and interact with others. What we say and how we treat others is important because we may be the only way some people encounter Jesus. So we must let our light shine in a way so that others can see Christ.

As you read this book, I invite you to pause, reflect, and immerse yourself in the divine love that surrounds and empowers you. Despite the trials and tribulations that life often presents, you can find delight and wisdom in God's words—an everlasting source of guidance, protection, and truth.

I hope that as you turn each page, you feel comforted, reassured, and inspired to deepen your relationship with God. Remember, you are never alone on this journey of faith. God's love is your constant companion, your guiding light in moments of darkness, and a source of unending joy and hope.

Blessings,

1 | CALLED AND EMPOWERED TO LOVE

Though I speak with the tongues of men and of angels, but have not love, I have become sounding brass or a clanging cymbal. And though I have the gift of prophecy, and understand all mysteries and all knowledge, and though I have all faith, so that I could remove mountains, but have not love, I am nothing. And though I bestow all my goods to feed the poor, and though I give my body to be burned, but have not love, it profits me nothing.

Love suffers long and is kind; love does not envy; love does not parade itself, is not puffed up; does not behave rudely, does not seek its own, is not provoked, thinks no evil; does not rejoice in iniquity, but rejoices in the truth; bears all things, believes all things, hopes all things, endures all things.

Love never fails. But whether there are prophecies, they will fail; whether there are tongues, they will cease; whether there is knowledge, it will vanish away.

1 CORINTHIANS 13:1-8

If I were to write my personal version of today's scripture from the apostle Paul, it would start something like this: "Though I work in the kitchen at every men's breakfast, though I pray in the empty sanctuary every morning at five thirty, though I have the ability to corral junior high kids during Wednesday night youth group, and though I run the soundboard whenever the need arises, if I have not love, I am nothing."

This passage reminds us that God cares much more about our hearts and what motivates us to serve Him than He does about our acts of service. Paul understood that the heart is what God looks at. People around us may see our deeds, but God knows why we do them. May we therefore do with love all we do for God.

Paul then went on to describe love. Read through the second paragraph of the scripture—slowly. Think about how Jesus lived out each attribute. Then ask God to show you which aspect of love He'd like you to focus on this week.

The 1 Corinthians 13 description of love is a tall order, but God—who is Himself love—will empower you to do what He has called you to do. As you receive His love, it will overflow and enable you to love others.

2 | LOVING MUCH

"There was a certain creditor who had two debtors. One owed five hundred denarii, and the other fifty. And when they had nothing with which to repay, he freely forgave them both. Tell Me, therefore, which of them will love him more?"

Simon answered and said, "I suppose the one whom he forgave more."

And He said to him, "You have rightly judged." Then He turned to the woman and said to Simon, "Do you see this woman? I entered your house; you gave Me no water for My feet, but she has washed My feet with her tears and wiped them with the hair of her head. You gave Me no kiss, but this woman has not ceased to kiss My feet since the time I came in. You did not anoint My head with oil, but this woman has anointed My feet with fragrant oil. Therefore I say to you, her sins, which are many, are forgiven, for she loved much. But to whom little is forgiven, the same loves little."

Then He said to her, "Your sins are forgiven."

LUKE 7:41-48

She was bold, this nameless woman known by all as a sinner. Yet her reputation didn't keep her from entering the Pharisee's house as he and his guests enjoyed a meal. She had a mission. Standing at Jesus' feet, holding a flask of oil and weeping, she "began to wash His feet with her tears, and wiped them with the hair of her head; and she kissed His feet and anointed them with the fragrant oil" (Luke 7:38).

The conversation in today's passage unfolded when onlookers were appalled that Jesus had allowed the woman to touch Him. He responded with a lesson on forgiveness. This woman was brokenhearted over her sin and then overwhelmed by Jesus' grace. He forgave her and delivered her from eternal separation from God, the consequence of sin. Her response to this unmerited favor was an extravagant expression of her love: she anointed Jesus' dusty feet with fragrant oil and washed them with her tears of gratitude.

Today, ask God to not only reveal to you the sin you have become blind to, but also—and perhaps more important—to help you appreciate the true nature of sin, of *your* sin. After this conversation with your Savior, you may find yourself loving Him even more.

3 | JUST AS GOD SAID

King Solomon loved many foreign women, as well as the daughter of Pharaoh: women of the Moabites, Ammonites, Edomites, Sidonians, and Hittites. . . . And he had seven hundred wives, princesses, and three hundred concubines; and his wives turned away his heart. For it was so, when Solomon was old, that his wives turned his heart after other gods; and his heart was not loyal to the LORD his God. . . . Solomon did evil in the sight of the LORD, and did not fully follow the LORD.

1 KINGS 11:1, 3-4, 6

God's command to His people Israel was clear: "You shall not intermarry with [foreign nations], nor they with you. Surely they will turn away your hearts after their gods" (1 Kings 11:2).

Five times in today's passage—"His wives turned away his heart"; "his wives turned his heart after other gods"; "his heart was not loyal to the LORD"; he "did evil in the sight of the LORD"; and he "did not fully follow the

Lord"—we read that King Solomon was guilty of exactly what God had warned His people about.

Remember that God had asked Solomon, "What shall I give you?" (1 Kings 3:5), and Solomon had said, "An understanding heart to judge Your people, that I may discern between good and evil" (v. 9). We see in this request that "Solomon loved the Lord, walking in the statutes of his father David," but the author of 1 Kings added, "except that [Solomon] sacrificed and burned incense at the high places" (v. 3). ("High places" were altars or temples built atop a hill where pagan gods were worshiped.)

Despite his wisdom, Solomon was not all in for God. We don't know if he stopped offering sacrifices after God blessed him with wisdom, but we do see that he intermarried—a lot! And there would be sad consequences for that unwise disobedience.

Our loving God's commands are for our good, but our disobedience can be costly and heartbreaking. We are wise when we follow God and walk in His will.

4 | GOD'S LAW: A GIFT OF LOVE

What does the LORD your God require of you, but to fear the LORD your God, to walk in all His ways and to love Him, to serve the LORD your God with all your heart and with all your soul, and to keep the commandments of the LORD and His statutes which I command you today for your good?

DEUTERONOMY 10:12-13

Do today's verses remind you of a New Testament passage? Perhaps it brings to mind Jesus' response to the scribe's query about what God's greatest command is. Of course Jesus responded without hesitation: "'You shall love the LORD your God with all your heart, with all your soul, and with all your mind.' This is the first and great commandment. And the second is like it: 'You shall love your neighbor as yourself.' On these two commandments hang all the Law and the Prophets" (Matthew 22:37–40).

To love God with all our hearts, all our souls, and all our minds means our honoring God, walking in

His ways, serving Him with all that we are, and obeying His commandments—which, as Moses stated in today's reading from Deuteronomy, God instituted for our own good.

Even in the ancient writings of the Torah—the first five books of the Old Testament, which are sacred to the Jewish people—we see God's love for His people. He provided His followers then and provides us today with guidelines for a good life. A life of obedience to His commands will honor Him and at the same time keep us spiritually healthy.

What amazing, life-giving love!

5 | RESPONDING TO GOD'S LOVE

"'You shall love your neighbor as yourself.' There is no other commandment greater . . ." So the scribe said to Him, "Well said, Teacher. You have spoken the truth, for there is one God, and there is no other but He."

MARK 12:31-32

In the book of Mark, Jesus taught that the second most important commandment from God is to love our neighbor as ourselves. What might this look like in your life? First consider the ways you love yourself: you spend time with people who build you up, you tend to your daily needs, you manage your money carefully, and you ask for prayer.

Now think about the people you'll see today. Which friend needs some encouragement? Which neighbor would appreciate your looking after her baby for an hour or offering to pick up something at the grocery store since you're going anyway? Is there someone at work you could grab coffee with just to check in? Could a family at church benefit from an anonymous monetary gift? Does someone need a reminder that you're praying for him?

When we obey God's Word, our light for Him shines brighter. So in our relationships—with family, friends, neighbors, coworkers, and even strangers—may our actions speak loudly of our love for others. Ask the Holy Spirit to make you aware of opportunities to love others in Jesus' name. You'll be blessed as you respond to God's love by sharing it with others!

6 | WALKING WITH OUR GOD

With what shall I come before the Lord,
And bow myself before the High God?
Shall I come before Him with burnt offerings,
With calves a year old?
Will the Lord be pleased with thousands of rams,
Ten thousand rivers of oil?
Shall I give my firstborn for my transgression,
The fruit of my body for the sin of my soul?

He has shown you, O man, what is good;
And what does the Lord require of you
But to do justly,
To love mercy,
And to walk humbly with your God?

MICAH 6:6-8

In today's passage, the prophet Micah asked a question that all of us have probably wondered: What can I do to honor the Lord and please Him? Thankfully, Micah answered that question with three of the Lord's requirements for His people. What kind of appropriate actions might you and I take in each instance?

- *To do justly:* What injustice could you respond to with God's justice? What local, national, or international injustice could you act against by making a call, sending an email, showing up at a rally, voting in the election, or sending a financial gift?
- *To love mercy:* Of all the world's many places where mercy is absent, which one most touches your heart? Does God want you to come alongside single moms or elderly shut-ins? Is He stirring in you a desire to serve the homeless or inner-city youth in some way?
- *To walk humbly with our God:* We who love Jesus are able to live with greater joy, peace, and hope than those who are doing life on their own. Start every day and repeat throughout the day, "Here I am, Lord. Please use me."

Humbly ask God, and He will guide you to where He wants you—at least for a season—to shine the light of His justice, mercy, and lordship.

7 | WALKING IN THE FOOTSTEPS OF CHRIST

If there is any consolation in Christ, if any comfort of love, if any fellowship of the Spirit, if any affection and mercy, fulfill my joy by being like-minded, having the same love, being of one accord, of one mind. Let nothing be done through selfish ambition or conceit, but in lowliness of mind let each esteem others better than himself. Let each of you look out not only for his own interests, but also for the interests of others.

PHILIPPIANS 2:1-4

As he clarified in Philippians 2:5, what Paul described in today's four verses is a God-honoring and Christlike servant attitude: "Let this mind be in you which was also in Christ Jesus."

This Christlike mindset yields like-mindedness, love, agreement, and unity with those who are brothers and sisters in the Lord. This oneness of believers offers a powerful testimony that the God of love we talk about is real, actively enabling us to love one another. Yes, we continue to be responsible for ourselves, to "look out . . . for [our] own interests," but not to the degree that we're blind or insensitive to the needs of others. We don't live as if life is all about us, because we know it isn't.

The chief end of man, as the Westminster Catechism teaches, is to glorify God and enjoy Him forever. And God gets the glory when we choose to set aside our own agendas and instead love others with His love, when we die to self and choose to serve, and when we work to bring peace and unity to the body of believers.

Encouraged by Jesus' love, inspired by His example, and empowered by the Spirit, we can humbly serve others and experience with them God-glorifying unity.

8 | KNOWN BY GOD

O Lord, You have searched me and known me.
You know my sitting down and my rising up;
You understand my thought afar off.
You comprehend my path and my lying down,
And are acquainted with all my ways.
For there is not a word on my tongue,
But behold, O Lord, You know it altogether.
You have hedged me behind and before,
And laid Your hand upon me.
Such knowledge is too wonderful for me;
It is high, I cannot attain it.

PSALM 139:1-6

Every human who has ever lived longs to be known and accepted. However, the fear of rejection often keeps us from letting ourselves be known.

In Psalm 139, David described being known to a degree that only our Creator God can attain. No one knows you as well as God does. The sovereign Sustainer of the entire universe knows when you sit down, rise up, and lie down. "Acquainted with all [your] ways," God knows how you do life and the path you are walking. Perhaps the most stunning fact is, God knows "altogether" the words you will say before you speak them. And the most sobering fact may be this: "You understand my thought afar off."

As much as David felt known by God, we don't sense any fear or nervousness in him. He clearly celebrated being known—and known thoroughly—by his Lord. When David wrote, "Where can I go from Your Spirit? Or where can I flee from Your presence?" (Psalm 139:7), he wasn't wishing such a place existed. Instead, he was praising God's faithful and constant presence with him.

David was aware of how well God knew him, and that intimate relationship and divine acceptance— available to you today—was a source of life-giving, soul-sustaining love.

9 | LOVING INSTRUCTION

Whoever loves instruction loves knowledge,
But he who hates correction is stupid.

PROVERBS 12:1

We humans don't know what we don't know. Oh, we may realize we'll never fully plumb the depths of Scripture or totally master a favorite historical era, a beloved classic, or a scientific mystery. But what about those subjects we haven't even heard of? There will always be more to learn. Our desire should be to never stop gaining knowledge and to remain lifelong learners.

Part of gaining knowledge is being open to correction. Granted, no one enjoys being corrected, but corrective truth spoken in love can be not only informative but also helpful, healing, and even lifesaving. Today's verse states that the one who hates correction is "stupid"—and the harshness of that word called for a little research. The Hebrew *baar* is defined as "brutishness,"[1] and another common English translation is *senseless.* But the use of the word *stupid* definitely gets our attention and may even remind us of a personal experience when hating correction did indeed prove stupid.

Clearly, to both love instruction and appreciate correction calls for humility before the omniscient Creator of the complex universe, the Author of all history, the Source of human creativity. May we humbly turn to God for wisdom and correction all the days of our life.

10 | GOD'S BROKEN HEART

"When Israel was a child, I loved him,
And out of Egypt I called My son. . . .

"I taught Ephraim to walk,
Taking them by their arms;
But they did not know that I healed them.
I drew them with gentle cords,
With bands of love,
And I was to them as those who take the yoke from their
    neck.
I stooped and fed them. . . .

"My people are bent on backsliding from Me.
Though they call to the Most High,
None at all exalt Him."

HOSEA 11:1, 3-4, 7

A heartbreaking passage to read, Hosea 11 tells of all God had done for His people Israel, also called Ephraim. He was their Savior from Egyptian captivity and their Redeemer who made the smallest of people groups a great nation. But these verses tell of Israel's response and how their choices impacted the heart of their Lord.

Anyone who has experience with children knows about kids' 24/7 demands as well as their significant milestones. God was there when Israel "was a child," and He was the One who "taught Ephraim to walk." God invested in His people, taught them well, and set them up for a life of rich fellowship with Him. Yet the Israelites turned to worship Baal and didn't recognize that God had been their Rescuer.

Imagine the pain of being rejected by your children and the sting of not being appreciated for all you've done for them. Hear what God Himself said: "My heart churns within Me; My sympathy is stirred" (Hosea 11:8).

Our loving God is a compassionate and patient God. May we not try His patience. May we instead walk in gratitude for all He has done for us—for His guidance, provision, and love.

11 | TALKING TO THE GOD WHO LOVES US

"In this manner . . . pray:
"Our Father in heaven,
Hallowed be Your name.
Your kingdom come.
Your will be done
On earth as it is in heaven.
Give us this day our daily bread.
And forgive us our debts,
As we forgive our debtors.
And do not lead us into temptation,
But deliver us from the evil one.
For Yours is the kingdom and the power and the glory forever. Amen."

MATTHEW 6:9-13

Many people have analyzed and written commentaries about the Lord's Prayer. For now, let's consider a few simple thoughts:

- When Jesus' disciples asked Him to teach them to pray, He gave them the words in today's passage. Why wouldn't we regularly pray them to our heavenly Father? We've been taught by the best!
- Jesus warned His disciples about praying to attract attention to themselves. Instead, He instructed, "Pray to your Father who is in the secret place" (v. 6). Just as Jesus Himself did, find that quiet time and a designated place where you can pause and be with the Father.
- "When you pray," Jesus continued, "do not use vain repetitions as the heathen do" (v. 7). Jesus' model prayer has a simple, straightforward vocabulary and is void of "vain repetitions."

Rather than making prayer complicated, may we pray as Jesus taught us to pray. Let's first approach the Almighty as Father, acknowledge His holiness, and then both invite and yield to His sovereign will. Next, we make simple requests, asking God to supply our basic needs and meet our essential need for forgiveness. We then ask God to protect us from temptation and from the Evil One. We end with praise for the amazing God we serve, embracing prayer as our lifeline to God.

12 | JESUS' SACRIFICIAL LOVE

"Unless a grain of wheat falls into the ground and dies, it remains alone; but if it dies, it produces much grain. He who loves his life will lose it, and he who hates his life in this world will keep it for eternal life. If anyone serves Me, let him follow Me; and where I am, there My servant will be also. If anyone serves Me, him My Father will honor."

JOHN 12:24-26

Jesus and His disciples had arrived in Jerusalem for Passover, the annual feast when faithful Jews sacrificed a perfect lamb in remembrance of God leading their enslaved ancestors out of Egypt to freedom.

Knowing His death was near, Jesus talked about it using terms His disciples would have been familiar with, but they didn't fully understand His point. Though Jesus' burial would look like the end, His resurrection resulted in the production of much grain in the harvest of Christian believers around the world and for centuries afterward.

Jesus invited His disciples to serve and follow Him. His promise that "where I am, there My servant will be also" surely sounded appealing. But after Jesus' false arrest, unfair trial, brutal flogging, and excruciating crucifixion, that invitation may have sounded different.

Jesus lived out His love by being like that grain of wheat in John 12:24, by letting go of life in this world, and by becoming a servant to the point of death. Pause to spend time before His cross with humility, awe, and praise.

13 | WHOSOEVER BELIEVES

"For God so loved the world that He gave His only begotten Son, that whoever believes in Him should not perish but have everlasting life. For God did not send His Son into the world to condemn the world, but that the world through Him might be saved."

JOHN 3:16-17

Key to our eternal destiny is our response to Jesus' invitation to *believe*. Specifically, we are invited to believe that Jesus is God's "only begotten Son," who died on a Roman cross, paying the price for our sin, and then was raised from death three days later. God's love is evident in His gift of Jesus, who experienced a brutal death . . . and a glorious resurrection. Will you believe?

Belief is not merely a nod to the idea that God sent His Son into the world not "to condemn the world, but that the world through Him might be saved." Believing that Jesus is the victor over sin and death requires more than intellectual assent. Genuine, eternal life-giving belief calls for a wholehearted, all-in response. Once we know the truth about Jesus' death and understand its spiritual significance, the only rational response to that divine love is our love. We show our love for God by making Jesus the Lord of our life and living in relationship with Him.

This relationship begins now and lasts throughout eternity. Without a faith-based relationship with Jesus, though, the consequence of sin is eternal separation from God. However, Jesus experienced that separation from God on our behalf so that we may enjoy His presence for eternity.

14 | FOUR HEAVEN-SENT GIFTS

L̲o̲r̲d̲, lift up the light of Your countenance upon us.
You have put gladness in my heart,
More than in the season that their grain and wine
*   increased.*
I will both lie down in peace, and sleep;
For You alone, O L̲o̲r̲d̲, make me dwell in safety.

PSALM 4:6-8

Light, gladness, peace, and safety—what precious gifts God bestows on His children. And this is only a small sampling of our faithful God's generosity. But the four gifts David mentioned in today's verses meet universal and timeless human needs.

Consider first the metaphorical battle between darkness and light. We can think about it in terms of lies and truth, blindness and sight, or confusion and clarity. Those who are committed to Jesus or are looking for meaning in life will always choose light, truth, sight, and clarity. God's countenance upon us provides the light we need and want.

God also puts gladness in the hearts of those who love Him, and according to David, this heaven-sent gladness is greater than the contentment that a fine harvest of grain and a season's good wine provide. Of course it is!

The warrior David also praised God for the gift of peace that enables sleep. Fueling that peace is the safety that results from God's vigilant protection of His children. Peace, sleep, and protection are lifesaving not only for soldiers on the battlefield but also for us amid the battles we face.

All praise to our God for blessing us with light, gladness, peace, and safety.

15 | GOD'S MERCIFUL AND GRACIOUS REACH

I was formerly a blasphemer, a persecutor, and an insolent man; but I obtained mercy because I did it ignorantly in unbelief. And the grace of our Lord was exceedingly abundant. . . . This is a faithful saying and worthy of all acceptance, that Christ Jesus came into the world to save sinners, of whom I am chief.

1 TIMOTHY 1:13-15

The apostle Paul had been persecuting God's people, rounding up and imprisoning fellow Jews who had proclaimed their loyalty to Jesus. As Paul headed to Damascus to continue this mission, God got his attention. A bright light suddenly appeared and literally blinded Paul. Then he heard the question, "Why are you persecuting Me?" When Paul asked, "Who are You?" the voice replied, "I am Jesus" (Acts 9:4–5). We may not have a salvation story as dramatic as Paul's, but the moment we recognized our need for a Savior and acknowledged Jesus as that Savior was supernaturally remarkable.

Considering his history of blasphemy, persecution, and insolence, Paul marveled at God's great mercy: he didn't get the punishment that was due him. Paul also marveled at God's abundant grace as he received blessings far greater than he deserved. Whatever our sinful past, our confession of our sins and our choice to name Jesus as our Savior and Lord means a fresh start, a rebirth, and the opportunity to journey through life as an adopted child of our God of love.

May Paul's salvation story—and yours as well—encourage you to keep praying for people and sharing the gospel. No one is beyond God's merciful and gracious reach.

16 | LOVING OUR DELIVERER

I love the LORD, because He has heard
My voice and my supplications. . . .

The pains of death surrounded me,
And the pangs of Sheol laid hold of me;
I found trouble and sorrow.
Then I called upon the name of the LORD:
"O LORD, I implore You, deliver my soul!" . . .

You have delivered my soul from death,
My eyes from tears,
And my feet from falling.
I will walk before the LORD
In the land of the living.

PSALM 116:1, 3-4, 8-9

Psalm 116 opens with a proclamation of love and thanksgiving. The psalmist wrote that when "the pains of death surrounded [him]," he "called" on the

Lord, who then "delivered [the psalmist's] soul from death." Maybe death threatened on the battleground, or perhaps the psalmist found his life spared from disease. Whatever mercy God showed him compelled praise and gratitude.

Now read today's passage from the perspective we have on this side of the cross, after Jesus' victory over sin and death, after receiving His gifts of eternal life and the Holy Spirit's presence within us.

What "trouble and sorrow" brought you to the end of yourself, to the awareness that you couldn't handle life on your own? What "pains of death"—figuratively speaking—did God use to help you recognize your need for a Savior?

Having acknowledged your need and accepted God's Son as your Savior, you can proclaim with the psalmist, "You have delivered my soul from death." Yet your salvation from death is far greater than what the psalmist knew: God has delivered followers of Jesus from eternal, spiritual death.

Confident that God hears our prayers, we can "call upon Him as long as [we] live" and then enjoy eternity with Him.

17 | GOD'S OPEN ARMS

"The sons of the foreigner
Who join themselves to the Lord, to serve Him,
And to love the name of the Lord, to be His servants—
Everyone who keeps from defiling the Sabbath,
And holds fast My covenant—
Even them I will bring to My holy mountain,
And make them joyful in My house of prayer.
Their burnt offerings and their sacrifices
Will be accepted on My altar;
For My house shall be called a house of prayer for all
  nations."

ISAIAH 56:6-7

In the Old Testament, Israel was rightly known as God's chosen people. God chose them when He called Abram to leave his homeland and follow Him. With this calling came extraordinary promises: "I will make you a great nation; I will bless you and make your name great" (Genesis 12:2). With those blessings came the responsibility to be a blessing to other nations: "In you all the families of the earth shall be blessed" (v. 3). God's people would shine His light and share His truth throughout the world. They would proclaim the wonderful news that God was going to send a Messiah to save them from the consequences of their sin, from eternal separation from God.

But what does today's passage hint at? Speaking through Isaiah, the Lord talked about foreigners, non-Jews, joining "themselves to the Lord, to serve Him, and to love the name of the Lord, to be His servants." God would "bring [them] to [His] holy mountain" and into His "house of prayer." God planned to "[gather] the outcasts of Israel" (Isaiah 56:8). Seven hundred years before the birth of Jesus—who rattled His religious contemporaries by associating with, preaching to, and welcoming non-Jews—God was already speaking about salvation for the Gentiles! What amazing grace! Gentile or Jew, receive that grace today if you haven't already.

18 | OUR FAITHFUL, LOVING GOD

The Lord is faithful, who will establish you and guard you from the evil one. . . . Now may the Lord direct your hearts into the love of God and into the patience of Christ.

2 THESSALONIANS 3:3, 5

"The Lord is faithful"—what a rich truth! Here in 2 Thessalonians we see, first, that He will "establish" us; some Bible translations say "strengthen." Life is hard. No one avoids hurts and disappointments. Everyone experiences pain and loss. But our faithful God will strengthen us and enable us to weather life's storms.

We also read that our almighty God will faithfully guard us from the evil one—the tempter, the liar, the distractor, the deceiver. May God's protection make us bold in Him and for His kingdom. May that protection give us peace when we step out in obedient faith. And may that protection enable us to hear God's voice more clearly.

We find one more blessing in today's passage. In verse 5, the apostle Paul prayed, "May the Lord direct your hearts into the love of God." Each of us knows how easily we are distracted from the things of God. We know too well how frequently our hearts wander away from our gracious heavenly Father. How wonderful that when we do wander, God is there to direct our hearts back to Him and His great love.

19 | OUR ROCK, FORTRESS, AND DELIVERER

I will love You, O Lord, my strength.
The Lord is my rock and my fortress and my deliverer;
My God, my strength, in whom I will trust;
My shield and the horn of my salvation, my stronghold.
I will call upon the Lord, who is worthy to be praised.

PSALM 18:1-3

Look at the way David described God in today's verses. You can't miss God's strength or the blessings that His strength means for us, His people. In fact, it is quite likely that you can reflect on your walk with the Lord and find many praiseworthy times when He was your Strength, your Rock, your Refuge, and your Deliverer. May those experiences of His great faithfulness encourage you as you consider the following questions:

- In what area of life do you need God's strength right now?
- For what current challenge do you need to be mindful that God is your Rock?
- What ongoing battle compels you to find refuge in the fortress of God Himself?
- From what wrong thinking, bad habit, or spiritual struggle with disbelief would you like God to deliver you?
- For what relationship, situation, problem, or decision do you need to trust God?
- In light of where you are in life right now, why is it comforting that God is your stronghold?
- Why are you glad today that you can call on the Lord?

Praising God for His past faithfulness fuels our confidence in His presence today and His power that is available to us. Our loving and gracious God will never let us down.

20 | AMBASSADORS AND ADVERTISEMENTS

This I pray, that your love may abound still more and more in knowledge and all discernment, that you may approve the things that are excellent, that you may be sincere and without offense till the day of Christ, being filled with the fruits of righteousness which are by Jesus Christ, to the glory and praise of God.

PHILIPPIANS 1:9-11

What do others learn about the Christian life by watching us? What traits of Jesus do they hear in our words and see in our actions? Are we being good ambassadors and effective advertisements for our Savior and Lord?

Paul's prayer in Philippians 1:9–11 identifies ways we can give God glory and be winsome witnesses to His goodness. First, Paul prayed that our love for God and for others would be more fully guided by "knowledge and all discernment." May we love in the ways God wants us to love. He will give us the ability to discern those opportunities and then act.

Second, may we do with excellence all that we do. May we be sincere rather than hypocritical as we live out our faith, and may we avoid disputes and unbecoming behavior that might offend our Lord or put off anyone watching us. We don't want to get in the way of someone coming to know Jesus.

Finally, Paul prayed that we would be "filled with the fruits of righteousness," with the fruit of the Spirit, who is abiding within us and is a gift from the risen Jesus. We are to be God's witnesses to a lost world. What we say and do might make a difference in someone's eternity.

21 | TRUST, FAITH, AND JOY

Let all those rejoice who put their trust in You;
Let them ever shout for joy, because You defend them;
Let those also who love Your name
Be joyful in You.
For You, O LORD, will bless the righteous;
With favor You will surround him as with a shield.

PSALM 5:11-12

Throughout the Old Testament, God is described as a fortress and shield, our rock and defender, and a refuge and shepherd. Those names of God invite us to trust Him to meet a variety of our needs, to protect us and guide us, and to be a foundation for life and a safe haven.

Each of these names also carries an implicit promise, and David himself saw the Promise Maker become the Promise Keeper. David experienced God as defender when the murderous Saul pursued him for at least four years (1 Samuel 23:7–24:22). David knew the Lord as his shield when Saul's spear missed him (1 Samuel 19:10), and when he was young, David knew the Lord's help when the stone he slung ended Goliath's life (1 Samuel 17:48–50).

Again and again David put his trust in God, and again and again God came through—in His way and in His timing. As David experienced the Lord's faithfulness, his own faith grew stronger and his joy more profound.

When we put our trust in God and experience His faithfulness, we can rejoice as David called us to—and we may find it easier to trust next time.

22 | IT'S ALL FAITH

Though I am absent in the flesh, yet I am with you in spirit, rejoicing to see your good order and the steadfastness of your faith in Christ. As you therefore have received Christ Jesus the Lord, so walk in Him, rooted and built up in Him and established in the faith, as you have been taught, abounding in it with thanksgiving.

COLOSSIANS 2:5-7

Our relationship with God began with a step of faith: we trusted that Jesus' death on the cross paid for our sins and that we are forgiven. Ideally, having joined with others who share our faith, we experience the blessings of community, of learning from one another, praying together, and celebrating God's answers. In faith we maintain a relationship with God, making time to read and study His Word, to worship Him regularly, to talk with Him and listen for His voice, to serve Him by serving others, and to live according to His values and commands.

Putting our faith into action, we turn to God to be our shepherd, our rock, our Father, our hope, our fortress, our friend, our healer, and our Lord. Living in faith also means asking God for wisdom when we need it, acting on the Holy Spirit's nudge to do or not do a certain thing, and even bringing our fears and frustrations to God when the unfairness of life and the resulting pain are overwhelming.

As we walk through life, may our faith grow with God's guidance, provision, and protection as we trust in His grace, His goodness, and His love.

23 | OUR GREAT GOD

Your mercy, O Lord, is in the heavens;
Your faithfulness reaches to the clouds.
Your righteousness is like the great mountains;
Your judgments are a great deep;
O Lord, You preserve man and beast.

How precious is Your lovingkindness, O God!
Therefore the children of men put their trust under the
     shadow of Your wings. . . .

For with You is the fountain of life;
In Your light we see light.

PSALM 36:5-7, 9

Psalm 36 is a joyful celebration of God's character that offers us a glimpse of why the songwriter David and believers through the millennia have "put their trust under the shadow of [His] wings."

How does one even begin to describe our infinite God? David referred to the biggest things he knew. He linked God's mercy to the heavens, His faithfulness to the clouds, His righteousness to "the great mountains," and His fair and just judgments to "a great deep." Today we might refer to God's eternal nature in terms of light-years or compare His profound love to black holes. The vastness of our God is impossible for the human mind to grasp, much less describe.

David also praised God's loving-kindness. Our compassionate God will not abandon us, treat us unjustly, or even give us what we deserve. Instead, He offers us kindness and grace, welcoming our trust and protecting us "under the shadow of [His] wings." Just as baby birds find safety from the storm under the mother bird's extended wings, we find refuge in our Lord.

Finally, God is the source of a meaningful life on earth and of eternal life thereafter. In this dark world, He gives us His light of hope, guidance, and peace.

How great is our God!

24 | CHOSEN TO SHINE

Work out your own salvation with fear and trembling; for it is God who works in you both to will and to do for His good pleasure.

Do all things without complaining and disputing, that you may become blameless and harmless, children of God without fault in the midst of a crooked and perverse generation, among whom you shine as lights in the world.

PHILIPPIANS 2:12-15

One day every person who has ever lived will recognize that Jesus truly is God's Son, the only way of forgiveness, the only source of an eternal life of blessing. You are privileged in that God chose you to recognize this truth about Jesus now. What impact will the reality of your salvation—of your receiving forgiveness for your sins and your adoption into God's family—have on your life?

The answer to that question is for you to work out "with fear and trembling" and in partnership with God. He takes great pleasure in you, His unique and beloved creation. By the power of His Spirit, He will guide you "to will and to do" whatever will fuel His joy in you. Whatever path He guides you on and wherever He has you serve Him, He will enable you to become more like Christ, His goal for all His children.

The apostle Paul offered a few tips to get us started. One is that we not be complainers or arguers. May we rely on God to help us make good decisions rather than taking the world's more popular and often easier options. The resulting contrast with "crooked and perverse" people who don't know the Lord is the reason we "shine as lights in the world."

25 | **WALKING IN GOD'S RIGHTEOUSNESS**

The Lord loves justice,
And does not forsake His saints;
They are preserved forever,
But the descendants of the wicked shall be cut off.
The righteous shall inherit the land,
And dwell in it forever.

The mouth of the righteous speaks wisdom,
And his tongue talks of justice.
The law of his God is in his heart;
None of his steps shall slide. . . .

Wait on the Lord,
And keep His way.

PSALM 37:28-31, 34

The word *righteous* refers to our being in right standing with the Lord. That happens when we recognize and confess our sin and then invite Jesus to be our Lord and Savior. Acknowledging Him on the throne of our life should impact all that we think, say, and do.

Today's passage offers specific ways we can live out our God-given righteousness. We can, for instance, be just in our interactions with others and, on a grander scale, help pursue justice for the least among us. We are also called to keep and obey the law of God in our hearts. Doing so will—by the power of the Holy Spirit—transform us, enabling us to speak God's wisdom and live by it.

The psalmist also exhorted us to "wait on the LORD, and keep His way"—the second part of this command being dependent on the first. As we seek God's guidance, rely on His constant presence with us, and look to Him for direction, we can be sure that He will "keep [us in] His way."

May our thoughts and actions always honor God and reflect our gratitude for His Son, our Lord and Savior.

26 | FIGHT THE GOOD FIGHT

Those who desire to be rich fall into temptation and a snare, and into many foolish and harmful lusts which drown men in destruction and perdition. For the love of money is a root of all kinds of evil, for which some have strayed from the faith in their greediness, and pierced themselves through with many sorrows.

But you, O man of God, flee these things and pursue righteousness, godliness, faith, love, patience, gentleness. Fight the good fight of faith, lay hold on eternal life, to which you were also called and have confessed the good confession in the presence of many witnesses.

1 TIMOTHY 6:9-12

Temptations, snares, lusts, destruction, perdition, evil, greediness, sorrows—the beginning of today's passage lists enemies that lurk in this world and some consequences of losing our battles with them. But Paul gave Timothy—and us—a call to action as well as a battle plan.

"Fight the good fight of faith," Paul wrote. Enemies of God and His people aren't going to wander away and leave us alone. Neither will they be distracted from the mischief and destruction they want to wreak. They are going to attack, seeming to know our most vulnerable areas and when we're at our weakest. Showing no mercy, our enemies can be devious and relentless. After all, they are intent on hurting God by trying to destroy His people.

But our choice to stay focused on our pursuit of "righteousness, godliness, faith, love, patience, [and] gentleness" will make us blind to the Enemy's lures and strong against any skirmishes he tries to initiate.

Furthermore, Paul called us to fight with faith, holding fast to the hope of eternal life with our Savior and Lord and standing solid on the "good confession" of who our God is, of His character, His promises, His blessings, and His presence with us. The victory is His!

27 | LIVING BY FAITH

I am not ashamed of the gospel of Christ, for it is the power of God to salvation for everyone who believes, for the Jew first and also for the Greek. For in it the righteousness of God is revealed from faith to faith; as it is written, "The just shall live by faith."

ROMANS 1:16-17

Having faith is secondary in importance to what or whom we put our faith in. Here, the apostle Paul spoke about having faith in God and told us two key facts about the One we Christians have placed our faith in.

First, God's power is evident in the salvation that Jesus made available to us by His death and resurrection. His victory over sin and death is the gospel of which the apostle Paul was not ashamed. Jesus took upon Himself the punishment for our sin and experienced the consequent separation from God—but our powerful God raised Jesus from the dead, defeating once and for all humanity's great enemies, sin and death. Clearly, no one is more powerful than our God.

These verses also declare that God is righteous. His unlimited power would be terrifying if not for His righteousness—if He used that power for evil rather than good, for destruction rather than salvation and new life. But His omnipotence is guided by His righteousness, wisdom, and love.

May we, like Paul, never be ashamed of the gospel. Instead, stepping out in faith and relying on God's strength, may we always take a bold stand for Him. Our lost world needs God and His love.

28 | WITH ALL OUR HEARTS

I said in my haste,
"I am cut off from before Your eyes";
Nevertheless You heard the voice of my supplications
When I cried out to You.

Oh, love the Lord, all you His saints!
For the Lord preserves the faithful,
And fully repays the proud person.
Be of good courage,
And He shall strengthen your heart,
All you who hope in the Lord.

PSALM 31:22-24

As we explore these verses from Psalm 31, we hear the voice of a man who is both very human and very devoted to his God.

"I am cut off from before Your eyes," David cried. Maybe you know that feeling. God is nowhere around, seemingly out of earshot of all your prayers. You feel forgotten and alone—yet the God who responded to David will also respond to you. Be encouraged by David's experience: God will make His ever-presence with you known; He will respond.

Then, perhaps resulting from his renewed sense of God's care, David encouraged his fellow believers to "love the Lord," the Almighty, who "preserves the faithful." By reviewing God's faithfulness, in big ways and personal ways, you will fuel your love for Him. Take a few minutes now—and regularly—to do so.

Finally, David's charge to "be of good courage" was spoken by a valiant soldier who knew great conflict as well as God-given success on the battlefield. Being confident of both God's faithfulness in the past and His calling on David's life for the present and future, David found the courage he needed.

Like David, continue to hope in the Lord even when you're not sure He hears you, for "He shall strengthen your heart."

29 | NO WORRIES!

"I say to you, do not worry about your life, what you will eat or what you will drink; nor about your body, what you will put on. Is not life more than food and the body more than clothing? Look at the birds of the air, for they neither sow nor reap nor gather into barns; yet your heavenly Father feeds them....

"So why do you worry about clothing? Consider the lilies of the field, how they grow: they neither toil nor spin; and yet I say to you that even Solomon in all his glory was not arrayed like one of these....

"Do not worry, saying, 'What shall we eat?' or 'What shall we drink?' or 'What shall we wear?' . . . For your heavenly Father knows that you need all these things. But seek first the kingdom of God and His righteousness, and all these things shall be added to you."

MATTHEW 6:25-26, 28-29, 31-33

Why do so many of us spend so much time and energy on the one thing that doesn't accomplish anything positive? I'm talking about worry.

We human beings tend to worry, and nothing—big or small—is off-limits. We worry about events in the headlines: global unrest, national politics, the environment, and the list goes on.

Closer to home, we worry about whether we'll be able to pay our bills, how many more miles our car will last, if our kids are making good decisions, and whether we're saving enough for retirement.

Other worries are more fleeting: Will I meet the deadline? Will our daughter pass her chemistry class? Will our son's birthday party get rained out?

Jesus is aware of our concerns and worries, and He said, "Don't!" He challenged us to consider, "Are you not of more value than [the birds God feeds]?" (Matthew 6:26). He also underscored the futility of worry: "Which of you by worrying can add one cubit to his stature?" (v. 27). But Jesus' strongest argument against worrying is that "your heavenly Father knows" what you need (v. 32), and He will provide for you. Let's focus on seeking first His kingdom—on serving, worshiping, and nurturing our relationship with God—and leave the details to Him.

30 THE LORD SEES, HEARS, RESPONDS, AND COMFORTS

The eyes of the LORD are on the righteous,
And His ears are open to their cry.
The face of the LORD is against those who do evil,

To cut off the remembrance of them from the earth.
The righteous cry out, and the LORD hears,
And delivers them out of all their troubles.
The LORD is near to those who have a broken heart,
And saves such as have a contrite spirit.

PSALM 34:15-18

The word *righteous* appears in the Bible 536 times, including its 142 appearances in Psalms and 85 in Proverbs. Clearly, God cares about righteousness—but what does that churchy word even mean? *Merriam-Webster* defines *righteous* as "acting in accord with divine or moral law; free from guilt or sin."[2]

In light of this definition, we know that God is righteous, so of course He cares about people's righteousness—and its absence. Being righteous, or in right standing with God, comes only after we acknowledge our *lack* of righteousness—our sin—and recognize that Jesus' death on the cross was His taking the punishment for our sin. Because of His resurrection—when Jesus proved victorious over sin and death—our holy God considers righteous those of us who have made Jesus our Savior and Lord. And throughout Scripture God teaches us how we are to live and interact with Him and with one another.

Sparing His followers an eternal separation from Him is just one blessing God bestows. David celebrated that God keeps His eye on the righteous and His ears peeled for our cries, and He responds, faithfully delivering us "out of all [our] troubles" and staying close to the brokenhearted.

31 | PROMISES OF GOD

Because you have made the LORD, who is my refuge,
Even the Most High, your dwelling place,
No evil shall befall you,
Nor shall any plague come near your dwelling;
For He shall give His angels charge over you,
To keep you in all your ways. . . .

"Because he has set his love upon Me, therefore I will
deliver him;
I will set him on high, because he has known My name.
He shall call upon Me, and I will answer him;
I will be with him in trouble;
I will deliver him and honor him.
With long life I will satisfy him,
And show him My salvation."

PSALM 91:9-11, 14-16

Psalm 91 is a treasure chest of promises for we who "have made the LORD ... [our] dwelling place." The psalmist declared we will experience no evil, and no plague shall impact us. God's angels will watch over and protect us. What a blessed life!

But life doesn't unfold that way even for the most steadfast believer, does it? In this fallen world we experience the evil of nature's typhoons and earthquakes. People hurt us with their words and harm us with their deeds. Addictions, drunk driving, and adultery can ruin the lives of dedicated Jesus followers. Viruses, bacterial infections, cancer, and other diseases end the lives of God's people. Headlines reveal unspeakably evil acts that affect believers and nonbelievers alike.

So what do we make of these Psalm 91 promises? We choose to find comfort in God's presence in the tragedy. We remind ourselves that He sees the big picture and that His ways aren't our ways (Isaiah 55:8–9). We cling to the hope of heaven, where there will indeed be "no more death, nor sorrow, nor crying. . . . [and] no more pain" (Revelation 21:4).

God's promises are real. And though they may unfold in a way we don't anticipate or understand, we can choose to trust in His goodness.

32 | **PRAISE THE LORD!**

The LORD is righteous in all His ways,
Gracious in all His works.
The LORD is near to all who call upon Him,
To all who call upon Him in truth.
He will fulfill the desire of those who fear Him;
He also will hear their cry and save them.
The LORD preserves all who love Him,
But all the wicked He will destroy.
My mouth shall speak the praise of the LORD,
And all flesh shall bless His holy name
Forever and ever.

PSALM 145:17-21

As these verses illustrate, Psalm 145 is a song of joyous praise. In virtually every line, David praised the Lord for yet another wonderful trait.

Let these lines guide you through a time of reflecting on God's goodness and faithfulness in your life:

- Think of an example of God's graciousness—of His undeserved favor—in your life (v. 17).
- Remember a time when you called out to God and sensed His nearness (v. 18).
- Reflect on when God saved you in response to your cry to Him (v. 19).
- Praise God for when He protected you (v. 20).

Now ponder what some of these verses *don't* say. "He will fulfill the desire of those who fear Him" doesn't mean God is your genie and every wish of yours is His command. God responds in His time and His way when you pray the desires He has planted in your heart, which therefore align with His will.

Similarly, "the Lord preserves all who love Him" doesn't mean that we who follow Jesus will avoid all pain, disappointment, heartache, and loss. It does mean that God will walk with us in such times, strengthening us spiritually, mentally, emotionally, and physically.

In these verses from Psalm 145, we find good reason to join David in praising the Lord.

33 | **A PROVERB IS A PROVERB**

*Wisdom is found on the lips of him who has
   understanding,
But a rod is for the back of him who is devoid of
   understanding.*

*Wise people store up knowledge,
But the mouth of the foolish is near destruction.*

*The rich man's wealth is his strong city;
The destruction of the poor is their poverty....*

*He who keeps instruction is in the way of life,
But he who refuses correction goes astray.*

PROVERBS 10:13-15, 17

Perhaps you've heard it said that proverbs aren't promises. A proverb is a general observation about life, but our misunderstanding that it's a *promise* from God can lead us astray. We cannot assume that our promise-making, promise-keeping God is breaking a promise when we don't see a proverb play out in our lives as we expected. You and I can save ourselves a lot of disappointment and even anger at God when we recognize that a proverb is not a promise.

Nevertheless, proverbs can help us live life well because they have proven true in general. For instance, "Wisdom is found on the lips of him who has understanding" is not always true. Yet the truth that understanding can fuel and support wisdom is helpful. The opposite—the second part of the verse—makes sense too: lack of understanding will lead to foolishness, not wisdom. And so, may we read this proverb and do the wise thing: seek understanding.

General observations about life can offer perspective and put our current circumstances or dilemmas into context. May the Holy Spirit within us enable us to discern the wisdom a proverb offers and then apply it to our lives.

34 | THE GIFT OF GOD'S WISDOM

Wisdom calls aloud outside;
She raises her voice in the open squares.
She cries out in the chief concourses,
At the openings of the gates in the city
She speaks her words:
"How long, you simple ones, will you love simplicity? . . .
Turn at my rebuke;
Surely I will pour out my spirit on you;
I will make my words known to you."

PROVERBS 1:20-23

Flowers, music, rain, human love, puppies—believers and nonbelievers alike enjoy these gifts from God. The term *common grace* refers to the joys and provision God has woven into the world that bless everyone on the planet. To some degree, wisdom is common grace. After all, humans often gain wisdom as they journey through life.

Although God may not get the credit for it, both believers and nonbelievers also gain biblical wisdom. People use such popular sayings as "A house divided against itself will not stand" (Matthew 12:25) and "The handwriting is on the wall" (see Daniel 5:5), but not everyone realizes their source.

Likewise, believers may offer godly wisdom to nonbelieving friends who receive it without knowing its divine roots. It's wise, for instance, to take one day at a time (Matthew 6:34), to do what you've said you would do (5:37), and to treat the annoying coworker the way you want to be treated (7:12).

But there's another kind of grace and, with it, another degree of wisdom that are available to God's people. Only believers enjoy the grace of God's indwelling Spirit, who provides wisdom, as well as His promise that we will receive wisdom when we ask for it (James 1:5).

In today's passage, Wisdom cries out for us to pay attention. Will you listen?

35 | WISDOM'S WORDS

Counsel is mine, and sound wisdom;
I am understanding, I have strength.
By me kings reign,
And rulers decree justice.
By me princes rule, and nobles,
All the judges of the earth.
I love those who love me,
And those who seek me diligently will find me. . . .

My fruit is better than gold, yes, than fine gold,
And my revenue than choice silver.

PROVERBS 8:14-17, 19

Key to understanding these verses from Proverbs 8 is knowing who is speaking. Identifying the *I* is essential to learning from this passage. These words happen to be spoken by Wisdom herself. Knowing that, look again at today's passage.

We first read Wisdom's assertion that she offers solid counsel, manifests understanding, and instills strength in those who turn to her for guidance and find confidence for life when they do. Imagine living in a world like the one Wisdom describes! What headlines would we not be reading if kings turned to God for wisdom and if rulers relied on divine wisdom when they issued decrees about justice? And consider what season in your life would have been different had you sought wisdom. In contrast, what was the positive outcome in a situation when you sought God's wisdom and followed it?

I encourage you to think about the other statements Wisdom makes in this passage. Why do you think Wisdom loves those who love her? What does seeking wisdom "diligently" look like in your life—or what could it look like? And why is the "fruit [of wisdom] better than gold"? Spending some time with these questions can fuel your passion for seeking wisdom.

36 | GOD'S LOVE LETTER

Hold fast the pattern of sound words which you have heard from me, in faith and love which are in Christ Jesus.

2 TIMOTHY 1:13

Composed of sixty-six distinct books—thirty-nine in the Old Testament and twenty-seven in the New—the Bible is amazing for many reasons. Consider that more than forty authors wrote this Book over about 1,500 years in three languages: Hebrew, Aramaic, and Greek. Comprising history, narratives, poetry, proverbs, and theological discourse, the Bible is ultimately an invitation to enter into relationship with the God who created us and loves us. No wonder God's Word is considered His love letter to His people.

Jesus Himself knew the value of God's Word, saying in Matthew 4:4, "Man shall not live by bread alone, but by every word that proceeds from the mouth of God." With Scripture being essential to our health and life, it's no wonder Paul exhorted us to "hold fast" to the gospel message he preached, a message he shared as an act of faith in its truth and out of love for the Giver of truth and those He wanted to hear it.

To please God, we need to know His Word and do what it says (James 1:22). Only then can "the words of [our] mouth[s] and the meditation of [our] heart[s] be acceptable in [His] sight" (Psalm 19:14). And only then can we be effective witnesses in this lost world.

37 | THE ULTIMATE ACT OF LOVE

Do not be ashamed of the testimony of our Lord . . . who has saved us and called us with a holy calling, not according to our works, but according to His own purpose and grace which was given to us in Christ Jesus before time began, but has now been revealed by the appearing of our Savior Jesus Christ, who has abolished death and brought life and immortality to light through the gospel.

2 TIMOTHY 1:8-10

Almost two thousand years ago, an amazing, miracle-working Teacher got in trouble with both Roman and church authorities who nailed Him to a cross based on false charges. Three days later He rose from the dead, enabling us—who are sinners by nature—to enter into a relationship with God that will last throughout eternity.

What remarkable, sacrificial love! After all, "scarcely for a righteous man will one die; yet perhaps for a good man someone would even dare to die. But God demonstrates His own love toward us, in that while we were still sinners, Christ died for us" (Romans 5:7–8).

It's no wonder "the message of the cross is foolishness to those who are perishing" (1 Corinthians 1:18). Yet this incredible and completely true account is the story of our salvation. Jesus went to the cross voluntarily and gave His life so that you and I might have our sins forgiven, serve the Lord during this life, and enjoy a heavenly eternity with Him. What amazing love and grace!

May we never be ashamed of this glorious good news! May we never shy away from sharing "the testimony of our Lord"!

38 | HUMBLED AND ABLE TO RECEIVE WISDOM

*"He who corrects a scoffer gets shame for himself,
And he who rebukes a wicked man only harms himself.
Do not correct a scoffer, lest he hate you;
Rebuke a wise man, and he will love you.
Give instruction to a wise man, and he will be still wiser;
Teach a just man, and he will increase in learning.*

*The fear of the LORD is the beginning of wisdom,
And the knowledge of the Holy One is understanding."*

PROVERBS 9:7-10

In Proverbs 9, we find Wisdom speaking, sharing practical observations about the choice to receive correction and instruction. All of us make mistakes, but when we're willing to accept correction, we will be better for it, and our mistakes are redeemed.

However, receiving correction isn't always easy, especially when it isn't spoken with love. Still, when we wisely accept the hard truth about ourselves, we may find ourselves grateful for and even loving the one who rebuked us (v. 8). Having been humbled and then blessed, we may also be open to gaining further wisdom (v. 9).

Proverbs 9:10, one of the best-known proverbs, declares, "The fear of the Lord is the beginning of wisdom." Fear of the Lord is acknowledging that He is God and we are not; that He is completely other from us; and that He is pure and holy, unable to tolerate sin. As the creator and sustainer of life, He is all-knowing and all-powerful, the sovereign King over the universe and all history. Humbled by who God is, we can receive the wisdom that He has and we need. May our awe of the Lord and our openness to His wisdom never cease.

39 | WISE COUNSEL

Through wisdom a house is built,
And by understanding it is established;
By knowledge the rooms are filled
With all precious and pleasant riches.
A wise man is strong,
Yes, a man of knowledge increases strength;
For by wise counsel you will wage your own war,
And in a multitude of counselors there is safety.

PROVERBS 24:3-6

Imagine doing something for the first time. You may learn all you can, do your best to understand the information gathered, and hope for wisdom as you get started. Though doing it alone may work occasionally, you and I can save ourselves time, frustration, and grief when, instead, we seek wisdom from people who have experience.

Think of a time when, despite knowing the value of wisdom, you chose to fly solo. At what point did you realize some wise counsel would have been good to have? What misstep, wasted time, or frustration might you have avoided?

Now think of another time when you knew the task was beyond your ability and you sought counsel from people who knew what you didn't know. In what ways did you benefit from wisdom gleaned from others?

There's no need to reinvent the wheel. Often, the things we're about to attempt have likely been done successfully before. So let's turn to the people God has placed in our lives and find strength in the knowledge they share. They can help us through whatever battle we're fighting, and we will find safety "in a multitude of counselors."

40 | THE GIFT OF GOD'S SPIRIT

What man knows the things of a man except the spirit of the man which is in him? Even so no one knows the things of God except the Spirit of God. Now we have received, not the spirit of the world, but the Spirit who is from God, that we might know the things that have been freely given to us by God.

1 CORINTHIANS 2:11-12

Perhaps the least well-known and therefore most mysterious member of the Trinity is God's Holy Spirit. Though God's Spirit traditionally has been referred to as the *Holy Ghost*, we must remember that the Holy Spirit is a Person, not an "it." This fact invites relationship, conversation, and trust. His very name speaks of approachability as well as substance. The Holy Spirit is a Person who knows our God and our Savior better than we do, and He longs to share that knowledge with us.

Paul offered further insight into the Holy Spirit when he compared the relationship of the spirit of a man to that man and the relationship between the Spirit of

God to God Himself. "What man knows the things of a man," Paul asked, "except the spirit of the man which is in him?" Likewise, the Holy Spirit "knows the things of God," and He shares those truths with God's people. We don't have to guess about who God is or what He wants us to do. The Holy Spirit who inspired Scripture also helps us understand that written Word and live it out.

As we have been blessed to receive the gift of the Spirit, may we learn to listen for His voice when we worship, study Scripture, and go about our lives.

41 | WHAT GOD ARE YOU FOLLOWING?

You shall not listen to the words of that prophet or that dreamer of dreams, for the LORD your God is testing you to know whether you love the LORD your God with all your heart and with all your soul. You shall walk after the LORD your God and fear Him, and keep His commandments and obey His voice; you shall serve Him and hold fast to Him.

DEUTERONOMY 13:3-4

Old Testament rivals to the one true God were often tangible—an idol carved out of wood, a gold-plated altar to another god, or a temple inviting immoral behavior. In the twenty-first century, our idols are subtler. We may, for instance, be enticed to worship the idol of that car or house or bottom line, that altar plated with prestige and adorned with the world's awards, or that temple we erected to ourselves.

Then and now, words of false prophets and deceived dreamers as well as idols, tangible or intangible, lead us nowhere good. Moses reminded the people of Israel that their God—the God of Abraham, Isaac, and Jacob—the one true God, deserved their wholehearted worship.

But life in this fallen world offers many tests of our loyalty. What keeps you from loving "the Lord your God with all your heart and with all your soul"? Ask the Holy Spirit to help you recognize when idols are trying to distract you. Then rely on His strength to help you turn from them and follow God.

Know, too, that being grounded in God's Word, worshiping Him regularly, and being committed to fellowship with brothers and sisters in Christ can also help you stay on the narrow, life-giving path of following Jesus.

42 | LOVE WISDOM

I have taught you in the way of wisdom;
I have led you in right paths.
When you walk, your steps will not be hindered,
And when you run, you will not stumble.
Take firm hold of instruction, do not let go;
Keep her, for she is your life.

PROVERBS 4:11-13

Among the many life-giving blessings the Lord has bestowed upon His people, the gift of wisdom is near the top.

Though perhaps not valued today the way it was in Jesus' time, *wisdom* can be defined as "knowledge of God applied well to real life." The father's words in today's passage reveal his respect for wisdom. He knew its value for his son.

Still, the concept of wisdom may seem esoteric and vague, far removed from your everyday dilemmas and decisions. If that's the case, take hold of the promise of

James 1:5: "If any of you lacks wisdom, let him ask of God, who gives to all liberally and without reproach, and it will be given to him."

May this promise make wisdom seem more within your reach and more practical for your life. Also, be encouraged that God's wisdom is wiser than the world's cheap imitations, and He will enable you to discern it clearly despite the noise and distractions.

As the author of Proverbs said to his son, "Take firm hold of instruction, do not let go; keep her, for she is your life." God's wisdom is indeed a lifeline in a lost and loud world.

43 | LOVE YOUR ENEMIES

"You have heard that it was said, 'You shall love your neighbor and hate your enemy.' But I say to you, love your enemies, bless those who curse you, do good to those who hate you, and pray for those who spitefully use you and persecute you. . . . You have heard . . . 'An eye for an eye and a tooth for a tooth.' But I tell you . . . whoever slaps you on your right cheek, turn the other to him also."

MATTHEW 5:43-44, 38-39

Jesus' contemporaries were stunned by His teachings. He spoke of obedience to the Old Testament law as a matter of the heart, not of mere outward behavior. This life Jesus calls us to is no less radical today.

The Sermon on the Mount offers key kingdom-of-God instructions. Today's verses from Matthew reveal the counterintuitive, countercultural, and ultimately revolutionary nature of Jesus' words. His simple, straightforward language sounded paradoxical. Even the Rabbi's twelve closest followers didn't always understand Him.

The religious leaders of His day understood enough to be angry and want Him killed.

Our response to Jesus' teaching should be not only to understand but to obey. When we rely on the Spirit, He will enable us to do the impossible.

As for this command to love our enemies, C. S. Lewis called us to get right to it: "Do not waste time bothering whether you 'love' your neighbor; act as if you did."[3]

44 | WHERE YOUR TREASURE IS

Now behold, one came and said to Him, "Good Teacher, what good thing shall I do that I may have eternal life?"

So He said to him . . . "If you want to enter into life, keep the commandments."

He said to Him, "Which ones?"

Jesus said, "'You shall not murder,' 'You shall not commit adultery,' 'You shall not steal,' 'You shall not bear false witness,' 'Honor your father and your mother,' and, 'You shall love your neighbor as yourself.'"

The young man said to Him, "All these things I have kept from my youth. What do I still lack?"

Jesus said to him, "If you want to be perfect, go, sell what you have and give to the poor, and you will have treasure in heaven; and come, follow Me."

But when the young man heard that saying, he went away sorrowful, for he had great possessions.

MATTHEW 19:16-22

Our holy God's gifts of forgiveness, righteousness, His indwelling Spirit, adoption into His family, and eternal life with Him are staggering in their significance. What did we do to deserve this extravagant, unmerited favor? Nothing—that's why it's called grace. "Not by works of righteousness which we have done, but according to His mercy He saved us," says Titus 3:5. We can't earn our salvation, but if we could, some of us might have an easier time receiving it. Consider the man in today's passage.

The rich young ruler asked what he could do to have—to earn—eternal life. Jesus first pointed him to the commandments, and the young man was confident he had done a fine job observing those. Was there something else? he wondered.

Yes, there was. Jesus knew what was keeping the man from acknowledging his need for a Savior: "Go, sell what you have." But he couldn't.

Jesus taught that "where your treasure is, there your heart will be also" (Matthew 6:21). The rich young ruler is a tragic case in point.

Ask Jesus to show you what is keeping you from being fully committed to Him. Then ask Him to help you address that issue as you follow Him.

45 | WILL YOU CHOOSE LIFE?

"I have set before you today life and good, death and evil, in that I command you today to love the LORD your God, to walk in His ways, and to keep His commandments, His statutes, and His judgments, that you may live and multiply; and the LORD your God will bless you in the land which you go to possess. . . . I have set before you life and death, blessing and cursing; therefore choose life, that both you and your descendants may live."

DEUTERONOMY 30:15-16, 19

God did not create robots and program them to always do what He wants and knows is best for them. Instead, God created human beings and gave us free will. We are therefore able to make decisions, draw our own conclusions, set our own goals, and chart our own paths even if those choices aren't good for us.

But God doesn't leave us in the dark about the potential results of certain choices. We don't have to guess what He considers best for us. In His Word and through the example of His Son, God has taught us how to live in a way that leads to abundant life on earth as well as eternal life with Him. He won't force us onto His path, but He assures us that His path leads to life, while other options lead to death.

We walk the path of life when we choose "to love the Lord [our] God, to walk in His ways, and to keep His commandments, His statutes, and His judgments." If that sounds like a tall order, remember that if Jesus is your Lord and Savior, you have within you the Holy Spirit, who will empower you to love God and obey Him.

Choose life and God's gracious blessings.

46 | LOVE BEYOND DESCRIPTION

I bow my knees to the Father of our Lord Jesus Christ . . . that He would grant you, according to the riches of His glory, to be strengthened with might through His Spirit in the inner man, that Christ may dwell in your hearts through faith; that you, being rooted and grounded in love, may be able to comprehend with all the saints what is the width and length and depth and height—to know the love of Christ which passes knowledge.

EPHESIANS 3:14, 16-19

You may struggle to put into words how much you love someone. Maybe you can't find a way to express how much a parent or grandparent means to you, what a blessing your spouse is, or how incredibly powerful your love for your child is. Paul may have experienced that same challenge. Here he prayed that the Ephesian church would "be able to comprehend . . . the love of Christ which passes knowledge." The apostle wanted believers in Ephesus to comprehend the incomprehensible, to know the unknowable. How could he even begin to communicate the extent of God's love to these faithful ones?

Paul knew that those believers would rely on the help of the Holy Spirit, who indwelled them, just as the Spirit does for us today. Paul set the parameters: he wanted this church to better understand "the width and length and depth and height" of Christ's love for them. The Holy Spirit could take it from there, giving believers regular experiences of God's gracious provision, providing clear evidence of His answers to prayer, softening hearts, or convicting of sin.

That picture of love speaks volumes.

47 | BE AT PEACE

In the LORD I put my trust . . .

The LORD is in His holy temple,
The LORD's throne is in heaven . . .

The LORD is righteous,
He loves righteousness;
His countenance beholds the upright.

PSALM 11:1, 4, 7

What do you regard as the most pressing international issue today? The threat of war? Lack of clean water for millions of people? Environmental issues?

Which national matter do you feel needs immediate attention? The economy? Illegal drug use? The disastrous effects of too much social media? Homelessness?

What pressing circumstances do you face in your own life? A medical diagnosis? Aging parents? The challenges of parenting? Job insecurity?

Today's psalm speaks to all three categories of concern and to every issue you identified. It emphasizes that God is on His heavenly throne, exercising His sovereign and absolute power according to His love, wisdom, and grace—yet exercising His divine power without violating our free will.

If certain circumstances require you to make a decision, talk to the Lord about it. He promises to provide wisdom (James 1:5), and He calls Himself our Good Shepherd (John 10:11). Whatever you're dealing with or concerned about, you don't need to face it alone.

Follow David's example and walk in the steps of generations of believers who have gone before you. For any matter, whether it be international, national, or more personal, put your trust in the righteous Lord, who, from His heavenly throne, reigns over all . . . and be at peace.

48 | THE BLESSINGS OF TRUSTING GOD

A day in Your courts is better than a thousand
  [elsewhere].
I would rather be a doorkeeper in the house of my God
Than dwell in the tents of wickedness.
For the LORD God is a sun and shield;
The LORD will give grace and glory;
No good thing will He withhold
From those who walk uprightly.

O LORD of hosts,
Blessed is the man who trusts in You!

PSALM 84:10-12

Consider a few observations about the riches of Psalm 84:

- Since God created us to be in an intimate relationship with Him, being anywhere with Him—"A day in [His] courts"—is better than anywhere without Him.

- God is "a sun and shield." The sun brings light, health, and growth, and the Lord does the same. A shield offers protection from the Enemy, whether a full-on frontal attack or a sly sniper shot. The Lord is such a shield. Being our sun and shield are just a couple of the ways God blesses us with grace and with favor we don't deserve.
- God's promise is amazing: "No good thing will He withhold from those who walk uprightly." However, we probably need to allow Him to transform our definition of *good*. What we deem good may essentially be what we *want*, yet we don't see the whole picture. God's idea of good is far more comprehensive. He considers whether something is good for us spiritually as well as mentally, emotionally, and physically. God will only give us truly good things.

Let us sing with the psalmist, "Blessed is the man who trusts in You!"

49 | GREATER THAN WE CAN IMAGINE

Now to Him who is able to do exceedingly abundantly above all that we ask or think, according to the power that works in us, to Him be glory in the church by Christ Jesus to all generations, forever and ever. Amen.

EPHESIANS 3:20-21

One of the many charming characteristics of children is their vivid imagination. They can paint fantasy scenarios in great detail and grandiose terms. Created by the young storyteller, beings in their world are able to talk, and they often demonstrate amazing strength and abilities. Maybe most significant, nothing is impossible in the worlds that children create!

As we get older, our imaginations tend to become less vivid, less colorful, and tamer, but in today's teaching about God, we find a challenge that appeals to our latent imagination. Speaking of God's omnipotence—His completely unlimited power—the apostle Paul wrote that God "is able to do exceedingly abundantly above all that we ask or think." Granted, when we are praying for our ideal jobs, our children's futures, a friend's healing, or the growth of our churches, we may think we are praying big! But here we read that God can do far more than the biggest and boldest request we bring before Him.

Furthermore, that unlimited power is guided by His unlimited knowledge, wisdom, and love. Your Creator not only knows exactly what will be good for you because He knit you together, but He is able to give you what will be good for you. What amazing love!

50 | JOY IN GOD'S WORD

Oh, how I love Your law!
It is my meditation all the day.
You, through Your commandments, make me wiser than
*   my enemies;*
For they are ever with me.
I have more understanding than all my teachers,
For Your testimonies are my meditation.
I understand more than the ancients,
Because I keep Your precepts.
I have restrained my feet from every evil way,
That I may keep Your word.
I have not departed from Your judgments,
For You Yourself have taught me.
How sweet are Your words to my taste,
Sweeter than honey to my mouth!
Through Your precepts I get understanding;
Therefore I hate every false way.

PSALM 119:97-104

With its 176 verses, Psalm 119 is the longest psalm. Given the topic, perhaps we shouldn't be surprised: God's Word definitely merits such a tribute.

Notice the impact that Scripture had on the psalmist. As one who regularly meditated on its truth, the psalmist was grateful for the wisdom, understanding, and protection that he found in his study. What he learned in his head translated into action: "I keep Your precepts"; "I have restrained my feet from every evil way"; and "I hate every false way."

But obedience didn't seem a burdensome, grit-your-teeth undertaking. Statements like "Oh, how I love Your law!" and "How sweet are Your words to my taste" communicate joy and delight.

Reflect on the time you spend with God's sweet words. What works for you? Reading daily devotions, attending a small-group Bible study, memorizing Scripture, or something else?

Also think about the impact of God's Word on your life. When have you been grateful for wisdom God provided through Scripture? In what ways has the Bible offered you protection? When have you found yourself delighting in God's Word?

May your life proclaim, "Oh, how I love Your law!"

51 | THE GIFT OF GOD'S WORD

Righteous are You, O Lord,
And upright are Your judgments.
Your testimonies, which You have commanded,
Are righteous and very faithful.
My zeal has consumed me,
Because my enemies have forgotten Your words.
Your word is very pure;
Therefore Your servant loves it. . . .

Your righteousness is an everlasting righteousness,
And Your law is truth.
Trouble and anguish have overtaken me,
Yet Your commandments are my delights.
The righteousness of Your testimonies is everlasting;
Give me understanding, and I shall live.

PSALM 119:137-140, 142-144

In today's passage we look at another section of Psalm 119 and its celebration of the Word of God. That phrase *Word of God*, however, doesn't appear in this section. Instead we find synonyms—*Your judgments, Your testimonies, Your words, Your law, Your commandments*—each of which offers a solid reason why we should study the Bible. But we need to know not only God's values, priorities, requirements, and guidelines, but also His voice.

Studying God's Word grows our love for our heavenly Father and for Jesus, our Savior and Lord. After all, the time we spend reading, meditating on, and memorizing His Word is time we're spending with Him. His Spirit uses that time for our good to renew our minds and transform our hearts so that we are more able to love selflessly and sacrificially as our Lord Jesus Himself did.

Consider, too, whether Scripture has impacted you the way it did the psalmist. What about God's pure Word do you especially love (v. 140)? Why is it significant—in general terms as well as to you personally—that God's Word is truth (v. 142)? What kind of understanding that leads to life does Scripture provide (v. 144)?

Take a few minutes to thank God for His Word.

52 | LOVING GOD'S TESTIMONIES

I hate the double-minded,
But I love Your law.
You are my hiding place and my shield;
I hope in Your word.
Depart from me, you evildoers,
For I will keep the commandments of my God!
Uphold me according to Your word, that I may live;
And do not let me be ashamed of my hope.
Hold me up, and I shall be safe,
And I shall observe Your statutes continually.
You reject all those who stray from Your statutes,
For their deceit is falsehood.
You put away all the wicked of the earth like dross;
Therefore I love Your testimonies.
My flesh trembles for fear of You,
And I am afraid of Your judgments.

PSALM 119:113-120

For 176 verses, Psalm 119 celebrates God's law, and its very design honors God in its excellence. Called an acrostic poem, the twenty-two stanzas of the poem align with the twenty-two characters of the Hebrew alphabet. Though we lose the scheme in translation, every line in a stanza begins with that stanza's Hebrew letter. Throughout the psalm are sprinkled various synonyms for *law*, words like *statutes*, *precepts*, and *commandments*.

The structure of Psalm 119 can make us marvel, but its subject matter should give us real pause. If we were asked to write out our praise for God's law, could we come up with even 176 words?

Jesus fulfilled the law, obeying it perfectly and teaching His followers that obedience is not just about actions but also about heart and motive. Even though the law was fulfilled by our Messiah, we should still be humbled by the fact that God is its source and by its call on our lives.

Psalm 119 sets the bar high for reverence for God's Word, respect for His commandments, and honor for His wisdom and instruction. May we say with the psalmist, "I love Your law"; "I hope in Your word"; and "I love Your testimonies"!

53 | **NO LONGER LUKEWARM**

I am Your servant;
Give me understanding,
That I may know Your testimonies.
It is time for You to act, O Lord,
For [the proud] have regarded Your law as void.
Therefore I love Your commandments
More than gold, yes, than fine gold!
Therefore all Your precepts concerning all things
I consider to be right;
I hate every false way.

PSALM 119:125-128

One phrase in Psalm 119—"I love Your commandments more than gold"—calls to mind Jesus' single-sentence parable of the pearl of great price: "The kingdom of heaven is like a merchant seeking beautiful pearls, who, when he had found one pearl of great price, went and sold all that he had and bought it" (Matthew 13:45–46). It is difficult to imagine valuing anything enough that we would sell all we have. As we examine this parable and today's psalm, may we be compelled to ask God to ignite in our hearts a passion for His kingdom, for His rule on earth, for His reign in our lives, and for Him to use us in His kingdom work in this lost world.

However, the psalmist's passion for God's law may reveal our own lukewarm enthusiasm. Living on this side of the cross, after Jesus has fulfilled the law and risen victorious over sin and death, we can seem much less passionate than the Old Testament followers of God.

If this is the case for you, pray to the Lord to give you that passion for all things that are of Him, for His kingdom and for His law that reveals so much about His character and values.

54 | LOVING GOD AND HIS LAW

Great peace have those who love Your law,
And nothing causes them to stumble.
Lord, I hope for Your salvation,
And I do Your commandments.
My soul keeps Your testimonies,
And I love them exceedingly.
I keep Your precepts and Your testimonies,
For all my ways are before You.

PSALM 119:165-168

"Great peace have those who love Your law"—and of course they do. God's law reveals His character as He takes a stand for justice, goodness, kindness, generosity, hospitality, serving, worship, giving to the church, sharing, stewardship, joy, gratitude, love, and pretty much every other positive trait we can think of. As we see God reflected in His law, we can know Him better and love Him more.

Our love for God and His law, however, is not merely intellectual or emotional. Love for God and His law *acts*: we are to live out what we learn. Peace comes with knowing what God wants from us, and we continue to know peace as well as experience His pleasure as we obey.

In other words, peace comes when we recognize God and His ways and then walk with Him as He guides. Our decision to follow Him is our decision to surrender our will to His will. This doesn't mean we'll be free of pain and loss, nor will life always be easy. But the path that God has for us—and that He walks with us—will always be good.

By the power of the Holy Spirit in us, we can indeed obey God's laws. We can love Him and love others, always for His glory.

55 | THE INSPIRED WORD OF GOD

You must continue in the things which you have learned and been assured of, knowing from whom you have learned them, and that from childhood you have known the Holy Scriptures, which are able to make you wise for salvation through faith which is in Christ Jesus.

All Scripture is given by inspiration of God, and is profitable for doctrine, for reproof, for correction, for instruction in righteousness, that the man of God may be complete, thoroughly equipped for every good work.

2 TIMOTHY 3:14-17

There is much truth and enouragement in the letter Paul wrote to Timothy, a brother in Christ and fellow servant of God. Prayed for by a faithful Jewish grandmother and raised by a Jewish mother, Timothy had indeed known God's Word "from childhood." So here, Paul charged Timothy to continue living according to all he had learned. The truth that had enabled Timothy to recognize Jesus as God's Son, as the perfect sacrifice for his sin, and as the victor over sin and death would sustain Timothy throughout his life of service to his beloved Lord Jesus.

The written Word of God is equally crucial to our own life of God-honoring service. Reminding us that "all Scripture is given by inspiration of God," Paul then listed solid reasons we should know and then do what it says. First, we have no surer source of doctrine: the Bible provides the solid foundation of our belief system and the principles that are to guide the Christian life. Scripture therefore offers grounds for reproof and correction when we stray from God's ways. And those holy ways—instruction in righteousness—are clearly set forth in Scripture.

God's Word equips us "for every good work," so let's do those good works wholeheartedly.

56 | SEEK WHAT IS GOOD

Seek good and not evil,
That you may live.

AMOS 5:14

As we go through life, we face many choices. Some decisions are clear-cut and easy to navigate. But even with those—and definitely with life's more complicated matters—we do well to turn to the Lord. He wants us to choose the good, and He will gladly be our teacher and guide. When we go to Him seeking His will, we live with a greater awareness of His presence and of His power and wisdom available to us.

Seeking physical good—being good stewards of our bodies—will enable us to live healthier, more productive lives. Seeking our emotional good will enrich relationships. Seeking spiritual good will mean learning more about our Savior, walking step-by-step with our Lord, and being transformed and led by His Spirit. Seeking God's good in our circumstances within our families, neighborhoods, offices, and churches will free us to serve Him always and well.

What a wonderful Savior is Jesus our Lord, who will shepherd us through life for His glory and our benefit. All we have to do is seek His good each and every day.

57 | A COMMENDATION

We give thanks to God always for you all, making mention of you in our prayers, remembering without ceasing your work of faith, labor of love, and patience of hope in our Lord Jesus Christ.

1 THESSALONIANS 1:2-3

What encouragement for the Thessalonians to hear Paul's gratitude to God for them! Paul commended them specifically for their "work of faith, labor of love, and patience of hope in our Lord Jesus Christ." Faith does indeed require work, love calls for labor, and hope necessitates patience.

Whether it's the work of believing even when prayers seem to bounce off the ceiling, the work of trusting when circumstances go sideways, or the work of choosing to believe the prodigal child is held in God's hands—we all would benefit from the acknowledgment that we're doing the work of faith well!

Then comes the "labor of love." It's easy to love the lovable, but what about the hard-to-love people in our lives? The demands can be great, and the cost, greater. Though we can become weary from the effort, God empowers us to love.

As for the "patience of hope," we can sometimes struggle to continue hoping. God's timing often isn't our timing. Yet when we ask for His help, He enables us to patiently, persistently hope in His goodness, power, and love.

By God's grace, we, too, can live worthy of commendation for our "work of faith, labor of love, and patience of hope in our Lord."

58 | THIRSTING FOR THE LORD

How lovely is Your tabernacle,
O Lord of hosts!
My soul longs, yes, even faints
For the courts of the Lord;
My heart and my flesh cry out for the living God.

PSALM 84:1-2

Unfortunately, familiarity can make us blind and numb to the many God-given blessings around us—including the blessing of intimate fellowship with the Lord Himself.

Often, new believers long to know the God of love, who gave His only Son to die on their behalf. They intentionally spend time reading Scripture, learning about Jesus, and praising their Savior and Lord. This worship feeds their soul in ways they never imagined. But fast-forward five or ten or fifty years. Is that longing still there? Is the passion still fiery?

Look again at today's passage and notice the psalmist's longing to be in the place and presence of the Lord. If your passion has cooled, ask God to reveal the reasons. And ask Him to make you thirsty for Him.

Also consider what you can do to rekindle your love for the Lord. Has your Bible reading waned? Has your prayer life dried up? Have you given up regularly attending church? What kind of music could you listen to, to encourage you? Whose company might be healthier for you? Would a small-group Bible study be helpful in drawing you closer to God and others?

As God works in your heart to grow your love for Him, be sure you're doing your part. Receive the life-giving love He has for you.

59 | A LABOR OF LOVE

God is not unjust to forget your work and labor of love which you have shown toward His name, in that you have ministered to the saints, and do minister. And we desire that each one of you show the same diligence to the full assurance of hope until the end, that you do not become sluggish, but imitate those who through faith and patience inherit the promises.

HEBREWS 6:10-12

The *why* behind what we do makes a difference. Washing the car, for instance, is merely a weekend task to cross off the list. But washing your daughter's car to surprise her while she's out of town is much less of a chore and may actually be fun. Similarly, washing the car for an elderly neighbor brings a different kind of satisfaction than scrubbing your own car. Serving to bless someone or coming alongside someone in need makes the effort a God-honoring labor of love.

The Lord sees and remembers that kind of labor. Likewise, God sees, remembers, and honors acts of love that minister to the saints, such as teaching Sunday school or ushering at church. He also sees into your heart, which means that making widgets at the factory, balancing debits and credits in the accounting department, cleaning up the toddler's third spill of the morning, or whatever else fills your daily schedule can also be a labor of love for Him. When we live for our audience of One, the work He has provided for us can be a labor of love. Perceiving it as such can make the effort not only less tedious but also more satisfying and fulfilling. There will be renewed energy when you're doing things to bring God honor.

60 | IMITATING CHRIST

Be imitators of God as dear children. And walk in love, as Christ also has loved us and given Himself for us, an offering and a sacrifice to God for a sweet-smelling aroma.

EPHESIANS 5:1-2

If you've been around kids in a healthy family, you know that wanting to be like Daddy or Mommy is very natural. It happens without any prompting.

In today's passage, Paul exhorted believers to imitate our heavenly Father. Clearly, loving as God loves doesn't come naturally. But let's consider what aspects we might imitate.

- God gave us His Son: Do you want to be more generous?
- Jesus came to this earth to serve: Do you want to be more of a servant?
- The Spirit offers His presence when we're hurting: Do you want to be more aware of how

others are doing and more available to sit with someone who's struggling?

Choose one way to be an imitator of God this week—then choose another way next week.

Echoing this command to imitate God is the call to "walk in love, as Christ also has loved us." Walking in love requires us to surrender our selfishness and let go of our own plans, rework our schedules, and put off meeting our own needs. Walking in Christlike love also means depending on the Holy Spirit to enable us to love others with God's gracious and generous love.

As we imitate Christ and love the way He loved, God can and will use us to bless others.

61 | AN APPEAL

I might be very bold in Christ to command you what is fitting, yet for love's sake I rather appeal to you—being such a one as Paul, the aged, and now also a prisoner of Jesus Christ—I appeal to you for my son Onesimus, whom I have begotten while in my chains, who once was unprofitable to you, but now is profitable to you and to me.

PHILEMON 1:8-11

Paul's letter to his friend Philemon, a fellow believer and host of a house church, has quite a backstory.

Paul had befriended a man named Onesimus, led him to faith in Jesus, and benefited from his company and assistance while Paul was in chains. The issue Paul needed to address with Philemon arose because Onesimus was Philemon's runaway slave.

Based on Paul's position in the church, he could have commanded Philemon to accept Onesimus, but instead, in an act of respect and even love for Philemon, Paul made a *request*: "Receive him as you would me. But if he has wronged you or owes anything, put that on my account" (vv. 17–18). Imagine being Onesimus and receiving from Philemon a welcome characterized by Christlike mercy and grace.

Perhaps you're finding the apostle Paul's example of making a request rather than exercising authority rather timely. You may currently have an opportunity to address a difficult situation with humility and gentleness. Speaking the truth in love can break down barriers, change hearts, and redeem relationships. Keep Paul—and Philemon and Onesimus—in mind the next time you have an opportunity to act in love and make a request rather than issue a command.

62 | PRAYER: A LANGUAGE OF LOVE

May [God] give to you the spirit of wisdom and revelation in the knowledge of Him, the eyes of your understanding being enlightened; that you may know what is the hope of His calling, what are the riches of the glory of His inheritance in the saints, and what is the exceeding greatness of His power toward us who believe, according to the working of His mighty power which He worked in Christ when He raised Him from the dead.

EPHESIANS 1:17-20

My friend Michael knows how to pray—and he knows what to pray. For instance, when asked to pray for someone's physical healing, he will also pray for that person's spiritual growth. When asked by a mother to pray for her son's deliverance from addiction, Michael also prays for spiritual deliverance and salvation. In today's verses, Paul could have undoubtedly prayed for the Ephesians' practical needs, but look at the amazing prayer he spoke over them instead.

Notice the spiritual blessings Paul asked God to bestow. Of course Paul wanted the church in Ephesus to have the jobs, food, and clothes they needed and the health they desired. But here Paul asked God to give them wisdom, knowledge, understanding, hope, confidence in the eternal inheritance awaiting believers, and recognition of God's great power on their behalf, the very power that raised Jesus from the dead. That power of God also "seated [Jesus] at His right hand in the heavenly places, far above all principality and power and might and dominion, and every name that is named, not only in this age but also in that which is to come" (vv. 20–21). What a glorious picture of heaven and of hope!

And the beautiful truth is that today we, too, can receive God's spiritual blessings of love and heavenly hope.

63 | KEEP ON KEEPING ON!

Then Joshua called the Reubenites, the Gadites, and half the tribe of Manasseh, and said to them: "You have kept all that Moses the servant of the LORD commanded you, and have obeyed my voice in all that I commanded you. . . . But take careful heed to do the commandment and the law which Moses the servant of the LORD commanded you, to love the LORD your God, to walk in all His ways, to keep His commandments, to hold fast to Him, and to serve Him with all your heart and with all your soul."

JOSHUA 22:1-2, 5

Joshua's address to his soldiers from the tribes of Reuben, Gad, and Manasseh showed how well he understood human nature. Joshua commended them for obeying God and then encouraged them to "take careful heed" to continue to do so.

Why did Joshua think they needed to be reminded to stay on the good path they'd been walking? They undoubtedly needed it for the same reasons we do:

Our hearts are prone to wander from God; we stray from His values and commands.

- We can be distracted by the world's offerings.
- We can marvel at—and be tempted by—how easy and how blessed the lives of nonbelievers seem.
- We can be deceived about the wisdom and benefit of the path we're walking.
- We can become physically tired—and tired of dying to self.
- We can choose to veer from the path and then tell ourselves, "It's not a big deal" or "Just this once."
- We find ourselves influenced by unhelpful—even ungodly—ideas, circumstances, and people.

Even if we've been doing well, we can't ride that wave or rest on our laurels, because the opportunities to love God and walk in His ways never cease. We are never alone in our efforts, though; we can always rely on His Spirit, the truth of His Word, and His people for support in choosing obedience.

64 | LOVE ROOTED IN FAITH IN CHRIST

We give thanks to the God and Father of our Lord Jesus Christ, praying always for you, since we heard of your faith in Christ Jesus and of your love for all the saints.

COLOSSIANS 1:3-4

Day in and day out, we who follow Jesus as our Savior and Lord have many reasons to give Him thanks. In today's passage Paul thanked God for the Colossians' faith and their love for one another, which had been reported to him by someone who was impressed by their clear witness to Jesus. The believers in Colossae were living out the truth Jesus taught in John 13:35: "By this all will know that you are My disciples, if you have love for one another."

Think about your home church, your small group, even your family. What would onlookers see there? What evidence of your faith in Jesus would they find?

What acts of love would seem to them beyond mere duty or obligation? I remember neighbors marveling at all the meals our church family brought us the first three weeks after our son was born. They were intrigued by the saints' abundant love for us.

When it's our turn to do that kind of abundant loving, we will know the blessedness of giving, the satisfaction that comes with obeying God's command, and the joy of being used by Him to draw others toward His saving grace and love.

65 | LOVE BEGETS GROWTH— AND MORE LOVE

Speaking the truth in love, may [the church] grow up in all things into Him who is the head—Christ—from whom the whole body, joined and knit together by what every joint supplies, according to the effective working by which every part does its share, causes growth of the body for the edifying of itself in love.

EPHESIANS 4:15-16

Let's take a minute to unpack these verses that may sound a bit like a riddle.

First, the local church is a body of believers, and Jesus is the head of every such body. Here, Paul spoke of his desire to see unity among believers and to have every member of the body contribute to their church's ministry. Such teamwork would, Paul said, make the church effort "effective" and, in turn, "[cause] growth of the body."

When we join with fellow believers to do God's work in this world, we grow in so many ways. For instance, we grow in the joy of giving, in appreciation of the gifts God has given our brothers and sisters, and in heartfelt wonder and gratitude for the opportunity to be used by God in His holy kingdom work.

And such growth, with the accompanying sanctification (meaning to become more like Jesus), enables us to love more freely and more extravagantly. We edify—or enlighten and inform—others and find ourselves edified when we love with the love of Christ in ways that catch people's attention.

Finally, note that "speaking the truth in love" seems to fuel the growth of the body, and the result of that growth is "the edifying of itself in love." Love begets love.

66 | HUMBLE LOVE

"If I then, your Lord and Teacher, have washed your feet, you also ought to wash one another's feet. For I have given you an example, that you should do as I have done to you."

JOHN 13:14-15

With today's reading we step into a dramatic scene near the end of Jesus' life. He spoke these words just after washing His disciples' feet. No servant was present in the upper room when they gathered for a meal, and none of the disciples had taken on that duty. So, standing up from the table, Jesus "laid aside His garments, took a towel and girded Himself" (v. 4).

The apostle John prefaced his description of the footwashing by saying, "Jesus, knowing that . . . He had come from God and was going to God, rose from supper" (vv. 3–4). Jesus could humbly do a servant's job because He had no doubt about His kingdom purpose. He was also completely secure in His relationship with God.

Then, after Jesus washed the disciples' feet, He said, "You should do as I have done to you" (v. 15). We can learn from Jesus' example that no act of caring for another person is beneath us. In addition, like our Lord, we can serve because we know that our kingdom purpose is to love others with our actions. And like Jesus, we also know that we're secure in our relationship with God and in His love for us.

67 | LOVE THAT ACTS

You who love the LORD, hate evil!
He preserves the souls of His saints;
He delivers them out of the hand of the wicked.
Light is sown for the righteous,
And gladness for the upright in heart.
Rejoice in the LORD, you righteous,
And give thanks at the remembrance of His holy name.

PSALM 97:10-12

Wise individuals have observed that the opposite of love is not hate but indifference. We aren't to merely shrug our shoulders at the evil we witness in the world today. As we read God's call to "hate evil," we are hearing a call to action. Rather than choosing apathy and idleness, we are to act as God's representatives to bring light to dark places, justice where there is wrong, and healing to people broken by sin.

As we battle on the Lord's behalf, we can be confident in His promise to preserve our souls and deliver us from "the hand of the wicked." Seeing that "light is sown for the righteous," we can trust God to guide not only our thoughts as we rely on Him for a battle plan against evil but also our steps as we enter the fray.

And what gladness comes in knowing that we are doing the Lord's work! What a privilege to know Him and to serve Him in partnership for His kingdom! And this is only one of the many reasons we have to "rejoice in the Lord . . . and give thanks at the remembrance of His holy name." His love enables us to love, and we can do so for His glory.

68 | LOVE YOUR NEIGHBOR

"A certain man went down from Jerusalem to Jericho, and fell among thieves, who stripped him of his clothing, wounded him, and departed, leaving him half dead. Now by chance a certain priest came down that road. And when he saw him, he passed by on the other side. Likewise a Levite, when he arrived at the place, came and looked, and passed by on the other side. But a certain Samaritan, as he journeyed, came where he was. And when he saw him, he had compassion. So he went to him and bandaged his wounds, pouring on oil and wine; and he set him on his own animal, brought him to an inn, and took care of him. On the next day, when he departed, he took out two denarii, gave them to the innkeeper, and said to him, 'Take care of him; and whatever more you spend, when I come again, I will repay you.' So which of these three do you think was neighbor to him who fell among the thieves?"

And he said, "He who showed mercy on him."

Then Jesus said to him, "Go and do likewise."

LUKE 10:30-37

Perhaps Jesus' most famous parable, His story of the good Samaritan was prompted by a lawyer who wanted to test Him. Of course, the lawyer knew the greatest laws—love God with all you are, and love your neighbor as yourself—but he wanted some specific information. "Who is my neighbor?" (Luke 10:29). At the story's end, the lawyer admitted that the man "who showed mercy" was the neighbor to the one "who fell among the thieves."

The Samaritan, a member of the race hated by the Jews—and the feeling was mutual—was the good neighbor. He was also the character in the story least expected to step up. The priest and the Levite knew God's law of love. Wouldn't they obey and stop to help even if it made them late to a meeting at the synagogue or unclean and therefore unable to perform an assigned sacrifice?

When have we been too busy to stop and show mercy to a person in need? Are there times we have pressing engagements or important tasks and think we just can't spare the time? Worse, are we simply blind to the people around us who are hurting?

We are blessed when the Lord gives us eyes to see and a heart of love to serve the people in need who are along our path.

69 | DOERS OF THE WORD

Be doers of the word, and not hearers only, deceiving yourselves. . . . He who looks into the perfect law of liberty and continues in it, and is not a forgetful hearer but a doer of the work, this one will be blessed in what he does.

If anyone among you thinks he is religious, and does not bridle his tongue but deceives his own heart, this one's religion is useless. Pure and undefiled religion before God and the Father is this: to visit orphans and widows in their trouble, and to keep oneself unspotted from the world.

JAMES 1:22, 25-27

The word *hypocrisy* has its roots in a Greek word that means "playing a part on the stage, pretending to be something one is not." *Merriam-Webster* has a very similar definition of *hypocrisy*: "a feigning to be what one is not or to believe what one does not: behavior that contradicts what one claims to believe or feel."[4]

Merely hearing God's Word without putting its truth into action and without following His specific instructions can easily lead to hypocrisy. We may be saying the right things, and we may faithfully hear God's truth at church, in Bible study, or on podcasts. But if we aren't acting on the words and ideas we hear, we won't grow. We'll also miss blessings God has for us.

So what does being a doer of the Word look like? Ever practical, James didn't keep us wondering. Before the chapter ends, he called us to bridle our tongues, to "visit orphans and widows in their trouble, and to keep oneself unspotted from the world." A few verses earlier, James also instructed followers of Jesus to "be swift to hear, slow to speak, slow to wrath" and to "lay aside all filthiness and overflow of wickedness" (1:19, 21).

Practice what you hear preached, and you'll be blessed in what you do.

70 | GOD LOVES ALL

If there should come into your assembly a man with gold rings, in fine apparel, and there should also come in a poor man in filthy clothes, and you pay attention to the one wearing the fine clothes and say to him, "You sit here in a good place," and say to the poor man, "You stand there," or, "Sit here at my footstool," have you not shown partiality among yourselves, and become judges with evil thoughts? . . .

If you really fulfill the royal law according to the Scripture, "You shall love your neighbor as yourself," you do well; but if you show partiality, you commit sin, and are convicted by the law as transgressors.

JAMES 2:2-4, 8-9

Today's passage from James is a clear example of God's Word serving as a mirror for us to look into and learn whatever the Spirit wants to teach us.

As you ask the Holy Spirit to open your eyes and help you see yourself accurately, look again at the passage. What are some twenty-first-century equivalents to "a man with gold rings, in fine apparel" and "a poor man in filthy clothes"? In other words, to whom at church are you inclined to give more attention or preferential treatment? Who are you inclined to avoid? Why?

Are you loving your neighbors at church—your brothers and sisters in Christ—the way you love yourself? Expand that question by including your family members, fellow pedestrians on the street, coworkers, management at the office, other soccer parents, strangers at the gym—you get the idea. Are you loving your neighbors as yourself?

None of us needs to be told to love the people we find easy to love. So again and again in His ministry, Jesus called us to love the difficult to love. James was also very straightforward: "If you show partiality, you commit sin."

Recognize your sin, confess it, receive God's forgiveness, and ask His Spirit to help you love with His love the hard-to-love people in your life.

71 | **WORDS OF BLESSING**

Finally, brethren, farewell. . . . Be of good comfort, be of one mind, live in peace; and the God of love and peace will be with you. . . .

The grace of the Lord Jesus Christ, and the love of God, and the communion of the Holy Spirit be with you all. Amen.

2 CORINTHIANS 13:11, 14

Did you notice in today's passage our responsibility and the promised blessing? We're to offer comfort, reach consensus, and be peacemakers. Then "the God of love and peace will be with [us]," and His presence will enable us to continue comforting, coming to agreement, and making peace.

According to these verses, the Holy Trinity can help us love in the Christlike way God calls us to love. Jesus extended to us the unfathomable grace of taking the punishment for our sins and dying on the cross, and He gives us grace to love the hard to love. He helps us to see them as His beloved children and to love them with "the love of God."

As 1 John 4:8 proclaims, "God is love." Our infinite God is unlimited in His love and therefore able to fill us to overflowing with His love so that we can love others.

The Holy Spirit within us makes us aware of opportunities to love with His love. The Spirit will nudge us to offer a smile and encouraging word to the mail deliverer, another shopper in line at the grocery store, or the person emptying the wastebaskets at the office.

Fellowship with Jesus, the Father, and the Spirit enables us to love others with the love the Trinity has for one another.

72 | FRUIT OF THE SPIRIT

The fruit of the Spirit is love, joy, peace, longsuffering, kindness, goodness, faithfulness, gentleness, self-control.

GALATIANS 5:22-23

Who among us doesn't want to live a life characterized by love, joy, peace, longsuffering, kindness, goodness, faithfulness, gentleness, and self-control? If you're thinking that sounds like a tall order or maybe even impossible, be encouraged by the first few words of this passage: "the fruit of the Spirit."

A rosebush doesn't produce roses by gritting its teeth and trying harder. Roses result from the bush's God-given nature. Similarly, the fruit of the Spirit appears in our life not because we're gritting our teeth and trying extra hard. Instead, the fruit appears because Jesus' Holy Spirit has taken up residence within those of us who have named Jesus as our Savior. As a result, we can display Christlike traits. We can choose to cooperate with the Spirit and align our decisions with the instructions of

God's written Word, but the Spirit does the heavy lifting when it comes to making His fruit manifest.

Think about someone you know who truly walks in the Spirit, whose words and actions are characterized by the fruit of the Spirit. That person is undoubtedly a person of integrity and contentment who shines forth the light of Christ. You will shine like that, too, as you live in step with Jesus' Spirit.

73 | REJOICING IN THE LORD

I will greatly rejoice in the LORD,
My soul shall be joyful in my God;
For He has clothed me with the garments of salvation,
He has covered me with the robe of righteousness,
As a bridegroom decks himself with ornaments,
And as a bride adorns herself with her jewels.
For as the earth brings forth its bud,
As the garden causes the things that are sown in it to
 spring forth,
So the Lord GOD will cause righteousness and praise to
 spring forth before all the nations.

ISAIAH 61:10-11

We may think of *happiness* and *joy* as synonymous, but they aren't exactly the same thing. Happiness tends to depend on circumstances. In fact, according to the *Middle English Dictionary*, *hap* means "luck, fortune, fate."[5] As our circumstances change, so can our level of happiness.

Joy, however, is rooted in something more stable than life events, the state of our relationships, or how well we slept last night. For followers of Jesus, joy is a gift of the Holy Spirit, who dwells within us. We foster that joy when we keep our focus on the cross of Jesus, on the infinite love, gracious forgiveness, and amazing victory over sin and death that the wooden instrument of torture—now completely transformed—represents. Choosing joy means choosing to focus on the good news of the gospel and its promise that we will spend a glorious eternity with Jesus.

When we struggle to choose joy on our own, perhaps because of life's circumstances, we can always ask our heavenly Father to help us battle the distractions and the preoccupation with life events. Then, remembering that we wear "the garments of salvation" and the "robe of righteousness," we can say with Isaiah, "I will greatly rejoice in the Lord, My soul shall be joyful in my God."

74 | WHITEWASHED TOMBS

Then Jesus spoke to the multitudes and to His disciples, saying: "The scribes and the Pharisees sit in Moses' seat. Therefore whatever they tell you to observe, that observe and do, but do not do according to their works; for they say, and do not do. . . .

"Woe to you, scribes and Pharisees, hypocrites! For you cleanse the outside of the cup and dish, but inside they are full of extortion and self-indulgence. . . .

"Woe to you, scribes and Pharisees, hypocrites! For you are like whitewashed tombs which indeed appear beautiful outwardly, but inside are full of dead men's bones and all uncleanness. Even so you also outwardly appear righteous to men, but inside you are full of hypocrisy and lawlessness."

MATTHEW 23:1-3, 25, 27-28

"Do what I say, not what I do." These eight words offer an accurate summary of Jesus' more extended message regarding the scribes and Pharisees. Standing before a large crowd, Jesus was just getting warmed up when

He told the people to do what the scribes and Pharisees taught, but not "according to their works."

Then, addressing the scribes and Pharisees specifically, Jesus called them out for their hypocrisy, extortion, self-indulgence, internal uncleanness, and lawlessness. Always welcoming deferential treatment and content to draw attention to themselves with their outward display of religion, the scribes and Pharisees were not showing the Jewish people how to obey God's commands; they were not demonstrating how to honor God with one's life.

Jesus also addressed the heart attitude of His kingdom people: "He who is greatest among you shall be your servant" (Matthew 23:11). Unlike the scribes and Pharisees, Jesus, the Suffering Servant, didn't just talk about that. He acted according to His teaching and gave us an enduring example of His servant heart. He performed the ultimate act of service when He died on the cross for our sins.

75 | DARKNESS OR LIGHT?

"He who believes in Him is not condemned; but he who does not believe is condemned already, because he has not believed in the name of the only begotten Son of God. And this is the condemnation, that the light has come into the world, and men loved darkness rather than light, because their deeds were evil. For everyone practicing evil hates the light and does not come to the light, lest his deeds should be exposed. But he who does the truth comes to the light, that his deeds may be clearly seen, that they have been done in God."

JOHN 3:18-21

Nicodemus, a Pharisee, came to Jesus with questions in the dark of night. He knew from Jesus' actions that God was with Him, but he was puzzled. Knowing why Nicodemus couldn't see clearly, Jesus said, "Unless one is born again, he cannot see the kingdom of God" (John 3:3). After untangling the riddle-like metaphor that he needed to be born of the Spirit, not again be born of the flesh, Nicodemus was still perplexed. What did being born of the Spirit even mean?

After preaching the gospel in the well-known verse John 3:16, Jesus spoke about belief and disbelief. The choice is binary: people can believe or not believe that Jesus is the Son of God. Said differently, people will choose either light or darkness. Jesus knew that people "loved darkness rather than light, because their deeds were evil."

"The light has come into the world," Jesus said to Nicodemus. Nicodemus had a choice, and we have the same choice today: Will we believe Jesus is the light of the world?

Even if you already believe, go to your Lord and ask Him to show you in what ways you might be preferring darkness to His light. Ask Him to cleanse and forgive you so you can shine brightly for Him.

76 | **RESURRECTION MAJESTY AND POWER**

Gird Your sword upon Your thigh, O Mighty One,
With Your glory and Your majesty.
And in Your majesty ride prosperously because of truth,
humility, and righteousness;
And Your right hand shall teach You awesome things.
Your arrows are sharp in the heart of the King's enemies;
The peoples fall under You.

Your throne, O God, is forever and ever;
A scepter of righteousness is the scepter of Your kingdom.
You love righteousness and hate wickedness;
Therefore God, Your God, has anointed You
With the oil of gladness more than Your companions.

PSALM 45:3-7

What helps us unpack today's passage is the wording of Psalm 45's heading: "The Glories of the

Messiah." Knowing whom the psalmist is describing, we can join in the praise.

Picture the majesty of our Messiah riding into the kingdom, robed in holiness and purity, shining forth God's power and love, and content in the victory over enemies that was won "because of truth, humility, and righteousness." The Messiah has defeated lies and deceit, pride and narcissism, sin and evil. No victory is worthier of our rejoicing!

Furthermore, the Messiah's throne "is forever and ever." His triumph over lies, pride, and evil is everlasting. He has eradicated deceit, ego, and sin in the heavenly realms for eternity. What a glorious image of His Majesty sitting on His throne, holding His "scepter of righteousness."

This image gives us hope for the present. Jesus the Messiah proved His ultimate victory over sin and death when His resurrection transformed the meaning of His crucifixion. That "power of His resurrection" is available to His followers today as we face trials, temptations, and the "fiery darts" of the defeated Enemy (Philippians 3:10; Ephesians 6:16).

The love that compelled Jesus to go to the cross means strength for today and heaven with Him for eternity.

77 | **HARD TRUTH**

"Do not think that I came to bring peace on earth. I did not come to bring peace but a sword. For I have come to 'set a man against his father, a daughter against her mother, and a daughter-in-law against her mother-in-law'; and 'a man's enemies will be those of his own household.' He who loves father or mother more than Me is not worthy of Me. And he who loves son or daughter more than Me is not worthy of Me."

MATTHEW 10:34-37

Jesus always spoke the truth in love. And He spoke knowing that division would result when some people who heard the gospel believed and others didn't. This most important decision in life—"Will I receive Jesus as my Savior who died for my sins?"—definitely creates a fork in the road. The two options mean two very different paths in life on earth and in life eternal.

Jesus came so that everyone would be saved (John 3:17; 2 Peter 3:9), but He knew that wouldn't happen. He knew that communities, friendships, and even families would be split as each individual either accepted or rejected Him. Having one's family members become enemies might be the cost of following Jesus: "He who loves [a family member] more than Me is not worthy of Me." Never should we choose maintaining a family relationship over being a disciple of Christ.

Jesus longs for His followers to experience unity in Him (John 17:20–23). However, He knows the initial step toward Christian unity can cause division when one person chooses to follow Jesus and another does not. We are to love that nonbeliever with Christlike love, but we must not allow that person to interfere with or draw us away from our relationship with Jesus.

78 | WHAT GOD HAS PLANNED FOR HIS PEOPLE

"Behold, I create new heavens and a new earth;
And the former shall not be remembered or come to mind.
But be glad and rejoice forever in what I create. . . .
The voice of weeping shall no longer be heard in her,
Nor the voice of crying. . . .
It shall come to pass
That before they call, I will answer;
And while they are still speaking, I will hear.
The wolf and the lamb shall feed together,
The lion shall eat straw like the ox,
And dust shall be the serpent's food.
They shall not hurt nor destroy in all My holy mountain,"
*Says the L*ORD.

ISAIAH 65:17-19, 24-25

Out of the ground the Lord God made every tree grow that is pleasant to the sight and good for food" (Genesis 2:9). Into that lush and beautiful setting God placed the pinnacle of His creation, a man and a woman. Apparently the three of them enjoyed one another's company and conversation—until that fateful day. Having believed the serpent and eaten the forbidden fruit, Adam and Eve "heard the sound of the Lord God walking in the garden in the cool of the day, and Adam and his wife hid themselves from the presence of the Lord God" (3:8). The downhill slide had begun.

Not only our world but also our relationship with God and our relationships with one another have been impacted by the ravages of sin. But as today's passage reveals, this present state is not permanent. Imagine a place where we no longer hear "the voice of weeping"! And that is only one detail about the "new heavens and . . . new earth" God will create. We read in Revelation that "there shall be no more death, nor sorrow, nor crying. There shall be no more pain, for the former things have passed away" (21:4).

Let us join with Isaiah in joyful anticipation of this magnificent eventuality, this glorious eternity.

79 | OUR GOD REIGNS

Oh, clap your hands, all you peoples!
Shout to God with the voice of triumph!
For the LORD Most High is awesome;
He is a great King over all the earth. . . .

Sing praises to God, sing praises!
Sing praises to our King, sing praises!
For God is the King of all the earth;
Sing praises with understanding.

God reigns over the nations;
God sits on His holy throne.

PSALM 47:1-2, 6-8

Like all of God's commands, His command—His call—to praise Him is good for us. For starters, responding to His prompt to look toward Him means looking away from the cares, difficulties, pain, and struggles of life. We remember that we aren't the center of the universe and that our time on this planet is not to be all about us. Looking to God Almighty, the ruler over all the earth and the author of all history, helps us take a deep breath, be more aware of His presence, and find comfort and peace in His closeness. Looking into His eyes of compassion and love can help us feel less alone, more seen and known, and better understood, and therefore stronger for life's battles.

Yet that wonderful peace can be interrupted by inner turmoil—our unsettledness, anxiety, fear, and impending decisions—and by externalities, like family, relationships, workplace issues, and national and international turmoil. News headlines can be the greatest stealer of our peace. Looking up to God can make a difference. Seeing that "God sits on His holy throne" can restore a sense of peace. Our supremely powerful King reigns over all that concerns us. Hallelujah to the King of kings!

80 | A LOVE THAT PRAYS AND REFRESHES

Now I beg you, brethren, through the Lord Jesus Christ, and through the love of the Spirit, that you strive together with me in prayers to God for me, that I may be delivered from those in Judea who do not believe, and that my service for Jerusalem may be acceptable to the saints, that I may come to you with joy by the will of God, and may be refreshed together with you.

ROMANS 15:30-32

Even the apostle Paul asked for prayer, as you can see from today's verses. We see in his request not only specific concerns but also his anticipation of being with fellow believers who loved God and him.

God wants us to pray regularly for each other. Consider the command to "bear one another's burdens" (Galatians 6:2). The best way to do so is to pray for one another. We don't always know the specifics, though, unless people ask for prayer, which is something Paul modeled in today's passage. He asked for the church in Rome to pray that God would protect him from nonbelievers, bless his ministry, and enable him to go to Rome. Having specifics like that can help us pray with passion and motivate us to persevere.

Paul's desire to go to Rome—one of his requests—was based in part on something we ourselves have experienced: we can be refreshed when we spend time with brothers and sisters in Christ, with like-minded people who, committed to the Lord as we are, share our values, pray for us, and love us with God's love. When God is present in relationships—and He's always present where two or more of His people gather—the time is refreshing. Let's offer each other a love that prays.

81 | A RESTORED RELATIONSHIP

So when they had eaten breakfast, Jesus said to Simon Peter, "Simon, son of Jonah, do you love Me more than these?"

He said to Him, "Yes, Lord; You know that I love You."

He said to him, "Feed My lambs."

He said to him again a second time, "Simon, son of Jonah, do you love Me?"

He said to Him, "Yes, Lord; You know that I love You."

He said to him, "Tend My sheep."

[Jesus] said to [Simon Peter] the third time, "Simon, son of Jonah, do you love Me?" Peter was grieved because He said to him the third time, "Do you love Me?"

And he said to Him, "Lord, You know all things; You know that I love You."

Jesus said to him, "Feed My sheep."

JOHN 21:15-17

This conversation in today's scripture was unlike any Peter had ever had; he was talking with the resurrected Jesus. The risen Lord made a point of having this personal conversation with the disciple who had three times denied knowing Him. What compassion and love Jesus exhibited in this moment—and what humanity Peter had revealed then. Though Peter had bravely followed Jesus after He was arrested, wanting to save his own neck, he stood at a distance and then, when confronted, claimed three times he didn't know Him.

So, three times Jesus asked Peter, "Do you love Me?" While that repetition may have been painful to Peter, each assertion of his love for Jesus counterbalanced each time he had denied knowing his Lord.

But let us not judge Peter. Instead, let's be honest with ourselves. How often do we, with our words or our silence, with our actions or our inaction, deny knowing Jesus?

Instead of denying Him, let His love be known through us by how we feed His lambs and tend His sheep. We—like Paul—can proclaim with our lives, "I am not ashamed of the gospel of Christ" (Romans 1:16).

82 | SEEING OUR SIN

O God, You know my foolishness;
And my sins are not hidden from You. . . .

When I wept and chastened my soul with fasting,
That became my reproach.
I also made sackcloth my garment. . . .

Hear me, O Lord, for Your lovingkindness is good;
Turn to me according to the multitude of Your tender
    mercies.
And do not hide Your face from Your servant,
For I am in trouble;
Hear me speedily.
Draw near to my soul, and redeem it.

PSALM 69:5, 10-11, 16-18

Among the roles the Holy Spirit has in the lives of believers is helping us recognize our sin. We often become so comfortable with how we're living that we don't easily see it. This blindness fuels pride that further separates us from our holy God.

In Psalm 69 David was well aware of his sinfulness and cried out to God, asking Him to bridge the gap between His holiness and David's depravity by forgiving his sin. We can practically hear the agony in the opening verses. David's grief and repentance were heartfelt as he called out to the God he trusted, asking Him to show David loving-kindness and tender mercy. David was confident that God would indeed "draw near to [his] soul."

As the words of the psalm also show, acknowledging our sin leads to another gift, that of humility. We recognize our weakness and sinful tendencies when the Spirit convicts us, when we read Scripture, and when we worship God in all His splendor. Humbled before Him is where we should be. Aware of His vast superiority, we more easily surrender our will to His will, trusting in His wisdom and His love for us and relying on Him to enable us to honor Him with all we are and all we do.

83 | WHO CAN BE AGAINST US?

If God is for us, who can be against us? He who did not spare His own Son, but delivered Him up for us all, how shall He not with Him also freely give us all things? Who shall bring a charge against God's elect? It is God who justifies. Who is he who condemns? It is Christ who died, and furthermore is also risen, who is even at the right hand of God, who also makes intercession for us. Who shall separate us from the love of Christ? Shall tribulation, or distress, or persecution, or famine, or nakedness, or peril, or sword?

ROMANS 8:31-35

If God is for us, who can be against us?" The apostle Paul wasn't expecting an answer to this question. You might be able to come up with quite a list of people and circumstances that have been against you. But whatever you put on your list, the truth is—in Jesus' words—"No one is able to snatch [My sheep] out of My Father's hand" (John 10:29). What a great picture our Lord gave us with these words!

Look again at today's verses from Romans 8. Read them out loud. Hear the implicit yet powerful truth—and hear it not only with your ears but also with your heart. Realize that absolutely nothing can separate you from the love of God, nothing you might experience—not "tribulation, or distress, or persecution, or famine, or nakedness, or peril, or sword." After all, God bought you at the exorbitant cost of His Son's shed blood, and He will never let you go. What amazing grace! And what a glorious, sustaining truth for the challenges of life!

84 | GOD'S EVER-PRESENT LOVE

I am persuaded that neither death nor life, nor angels nor principalities nor powers, nor things present nor things to come, nor height nor depth, nor any other created thing, shall be able to separate us from the love of God which is in Christ Jesus our Lord.

ROMANS 8:38-39

What dream would you pursue, what risk would you take, what change would you make, or what relationship would you invest in if you knew that Someone who loved you so much that He died for you would walk with you every step of the way? Well, that Someone is Jesus, and His promise to be with you always is emphasized in today's scripture.

Of course, your answer to "What would you do?" must not be anything immoral, irresponsible, or foolhardy. God will still be with you, and He will still love you, but choosing anything you know is wrong devalues His love for you and cheapens His grace.

Consider now a deeper meaning to the Romans 8 promise. As you've surely noticed, life is difficult, and dark times can make us wonder where God is and whether He hears us, cares about us, or even loves us. That's when we must remind our hearts of the truth of Scripture: nothing we experience, no circumstances we find ourselves in, can come between God and us. His love for us doesn't waver even though our perception of it may. Cling to this glorious truth and praise God for the gift of His guiding, empowering, and constant love!

85 | "I AM THE LORD YOUR GOD"

"If a stranger dwells with you in your land, you shall not mistreat him. . . . You shall love him as yourself; for you were strangers in the land of Egypt: I am the Lord your God."

LEVITICUS 19:33-34

Fifteen times in Leviticus 19, God declared, "I am the Lord." In today's passage, that statement provides the context for His command to the Jews to love the strangers among them. God wasn't inviting discussion; He was calling for obedience. He also reminded the people of Israel that they themselves had once been strangers in a foreign land. Knowing what that experience was like would encourage them to extend compassion and love to any stranger in their midst.

But that reminder pales in comparison to the primary reason to obey God: "I am the Lord your God." In what area of your life—in what relationship, in what work situation, in what family concern, in what call to spiritual growth—is God saying to you, "I am the Lord your God," but you'd rather discuss the matter than just obey? *Does God really understand what His lordship in those circumstances will require of me? Does He understand how hard it is for me to trust Him? What if the outcome He wants isn't what I want?*

When we choose to live with Jesus as Lord, we need to remind ourselves of His goodness, wisdom, faithfulness, and love—and take simple but not always easy steps of obedience.

86 | A GENEROUS EYE

He who has a generous eye will be blessed,
For he gives of his bread to the poor.

PROVERBS 22:9

Imagine walking through life with "a generous eye"—with the ability to recognize opportunities to love with Christlike love, to help those in need, and to bless others with the treasure God has blessed us with.

Such generosity grows as the Holy Spirit works in our hearts to transform us, but our minds also play a role. Generosity comes more easily when we understand and remember that all we have belongs to God; we are simply stewards or caretakers of it. Our possessions are for us to use as He leads us. Opportunities are all around us—if we have eyes to see. This proverb nudges us to see with the Lord's eyes of love so we don't overlook people to whom we can give of our bread in Jesus' name.

And what about the promise that those with "a generous eye will be blessed"? We can experience the blessing of contentment that comes with obeying our Lord's commands. We can also live in the counter-cultural reality that "it is more blessed to give than to receive" (Acts 20:35).

Keep your eyes open so you don't miss the joy of blessing others with the blessings God has entrusted to you.

87 | A SOFT ANSWER

A soft answer turns away wrath,
But a harsh word stirs up anger.
The tongue of the wise uses knowledge rightly,
But the mouth of fools pours forth foolishness.
The eyes of the LORD are in every place,
Keeping watch on the evil and the good.
A wholesome tongue is a tree of life,
But perverseness in it breaks the spirit.

PROVERBS 15:1-4

Harsh words that stir up anger often come much more naturally than a soft, humble comment that "turns away wrath." And our tongues don't always rightly speak forth the knowledge we have. We are definitely works in progress when it comes to having a "wholesome tongue" that speaks life-giving words that encourage rather than wound or even cripple.

So what are we to do, since we often struggle to do

what we want to do and vice versa, just as the apostle Paul did (Romans 7:19–20)?

Our first response should be prayer, that gift from our God who truly wants to be in relationship with each of us. Jesus took the punishment for our sin and thereby bridged the gap between holy God and sinful us. So now we are blessed by His love and grace.

Because He loves us and wants what's best for us, our good and gracious God provided not only His written Word with His instructions for life, but also His own Spirit, who enables us to be obedient doers of the Word, not just hearers (James 1:22). God can and will enable us to speak soft answers, to use our tongues wisely, and to speak words that give life.

88 | ALWAYS IN MY PRAYERS

I thank my God, making mention of you always in my prayers, hearing of your love and faith which you have toward the Lord Jesus and toward all the saints. . . . We have great joy and consolation in your love, because the hearts of the saints have been refreshed by you, brother.

PHILEMON 1:4-5, 7

Imagine being Philemon and hearing these words of respect and honor from Paul, the person who introduced you to Jesus Christ and to the possibility of forgiveness and salvation! As we read this, we might wonder exactly how Philemon's life demonstrated his love for Jesus and faith in Him. Likewise, what did Philemon do to extend that love to fellow believers?

But perhaps we should ask these questions of ourselves: What in our lives demonstrates our love for Jesus and our faith in Him? What can we do to extend that love to our fellow believers? What words and deeds might earn us not merely the praise of a church leader, but the commendation of our Lord and Savior?

Paul's example for us is clear: he prayed for Philemon, mentioning him "always in [his] prayers." Are we praying "always" or even consistently for our brothers and sisters in Christ? Praying for someone is a significant way to love that person, and if you've ever been aware of someone praying for you, then you know the joy, consolation, and refreshment those prayers bring. Take a few minutes now to pray for a fellow believer. What a joy that we can be a blessing in this way!

89 | LOVE: A PARADIGM SHIFTER

Let all that you do be done with love.

1 CORINTHIANS 16:14

As a pastor friend is fond of saying, "In Greek *all* means 'all.'" In that case, the apostle Paul was making quite the statement here. All—every one of our tasks, chores, assignments, and responsibilities, every single action we undertake—is to be an expression of love. But how?

Perhaps you've heard of Brother Lawrence, the seventeenth-century author of *The Practice of the Presence of God*. As he peeled potatoes and repaired sandals, he did so with a keen awareness of God's presence with him and love for him. "We can do little things for God," Lawrence wrote. "I turn the cake that is frying on the pan for love of him."[6]

Doing things for others because we love God is a way to live out a selfless, sacrificial love. This kind of humble, Christlike love can greatly impact not only the recipient of the love but us as well. After all, when we are doing something with God's love, that perspective redeems the lawn mowing, diaper changing, grocery shopping, time-keeping, deadline meeting—it even redeems our dealing with hard-to-love people.

Practicing the presence of God by doing all things with His love—why not give it a try this week? You just may get a taste of how much joy this paradigm shift can bring.

90 | OUR HELPER, HAPPINESS, AND HOPE

Happy is he who has the God of Jacob for his help,
Whose hope is in the LORD his God,
Who made heaven and earth,
The sea, and all that is in them;
Who keeps truth forever,
Who executes justice for the oppressed,
Who gives food to the hungry.
The LORD gives freedom to the prisoners.

The LORD opens the eyes of the blind;
The LORD raises those who are bowed down;
The LORD loves the righteous.

PSALM 146:5-8

We see today in Psalm 146 the many ways God is our Helper: He is the keeper of truth and the administrator of justice. He feeds the hungry and frees the prisoners. He enables the blind to recognize Him, and He comes alongside to encourage and assist the heavy-laden. He shows us His love in many ways.

Living with God's Son as our Lord is key to the happiness and the hope the psalmist wrote about. Jesus offers the only hope that won't let us down. People, wealth, career, status, achievements, vacations, possessions—these will never satisfy our desire for hope, purpose, and significance. Neither will they provide happiness that lasts. Vacations end, careers fizzle, the market crashes, and children disappoint. But Jesus, resurrected from the dead and opening the gates of heaven for us, gives us reason for joy no matter our circumstances.

We also find hope and happiness when we base our lives on God's truth. We find in Him spiritual nourishment as well as His provision for our physical needs. He frees us from loneliness, brokenness, and woundedness, and He is always ready to give strength and wisdom when life's demands intensify.

The Lord is our true Helper, Happiness, and Hope.

91 | FAITH IN TIMES OF TROUBLE

Having been justified by faith, we have peace with God through our Lord Jesus Christ. . . . Not only that, but we also glory in tribulations, knowing that tribulation produces perseverance; and perseverance, character; and character, hope. Now hope does not disappoint, because the love of God has been poured out in our hearts by the Holy Spirit who was given to us.

ROMANS 5:1, 3-5

A life of faith in Jesus doesn't mean a life without struggles, pain, and loss. A life of faith in Jesus does mean, however, that we aren't in those tough times alone and that those trials can actually bear good fruit in our lives. God won't waste the hard times we go through. Instead, He'll use them for our good, as today's passage shows.

These verses first celebrate our justification by faith. Jesus took upon Himself both our sin and the punishment for that sin. He was crucified, but three days later

He rose from the dead, victorious over sin and death. When we put our faith in the truth that Jesus is the sacrifice God provided to pay for our sins, God accepts us as if we've never sinned.

Another glorious truth is that life's tribulations aren't for naught. God uses them to build in us perseverance for the journey of faith, a more Christlike character, and hope that doesn't disappoint because "we know how dearly God loves us, because he has given us the Holy Spirit to fill our hearts with his love" (Romans 5:5 NLT).

Assured of God's love because of Jesus' gift of His Holy Spirit, we can indeed "glory in tribulations" and live with hope that "does not disappoint."

92 | THE LOVE OF A JEALOUS GOD

"For My name's sake I will defer My anger,
And for My praise I will restrain it from you,
So that I do not cut you off.
Behold, I have refined you, but not as silver;
I have tested you in the furnace of affliction.
For My own sake, for My own sake, I will do it;
For how should My name be profaned?
And I will not give My glory to another."

ISAIAH 48:9-11

Today's verses offer us something of a cautionary tale. We get a glimpse of God's response when His people turn away from Him and worship false gods.

Of course God was angry, but in this instance He controlled that anger, choosing to "defer" it and "restrain it" from His people Israel. On other occasions, His anger with His wayward people played out differently—with a worldwide flood and defeat by enemy armies. But this time He did not "cut . . . off" His people. Instead He used the circumstances to refine them, to burn away impurities that interfered with their commitment to Him, to grow their knowledge of Him, and to strengthen their faith.

Such times aren't easy or fun for God's people. Knowing this, our compassionate God proceeds anyway—and He explains why. He lets us experience refining fires because He wants true followers who worship Him alone and who thank Him for protection and provision, guidance and grace. He doesn't want His people crediting the good in their lives to their false gods. God declares, "I will not give My glory to another."

Life's refining fires are uncomfortable, but God keeps us there until He can see His reflection in us more clearly, so He gets the glory for the blessings He gives us.

93 | THE GOODNESS OF THE LORD

The earth is full of the goodness of the LORD.

By the word of the LORD the heavens were made,
And all the host of them by the breath of His mouth.
He gathers the waters of the sea together as a heap;
He lays up the deep in storehouses.

Let all the earth fear the LORD;
Let all the inhabitants of the world stand in awe of Him.
For He spoke, and it was done;
He commanded, and it stood fast.

PSALM 33:5-9

What comes to mind when you read, "The earth is full of the goodness of the LORD"? What evidence of God's goodness does His creation—the heavens and the seas—reveal to you?

God's creation reveals much about Him. We see His creativity in platypuses, golden retrievers, and tarantulas as well as in blueberries, roses, snowflakes, and the human body. We marvel at the power of the wind and the water, the power contained in an atom, and the power demonstrated by elephants, blue whales, lions, and (look it up!) dung beetles, all of which which He crafted.

We appreciate the order and design of the universe He made. Even the fact that the earth has been dubbed the Goldilocks planet speaks to His perfect power in that it's not too close to the sun or too far from the sun; its location is just right to support life.

God's creation reveals His faithfulness in that He sustains this world He designed and created. We see His faithfulness in the recurring seasons we experience. We see His constancy in the constellations in the heavens.

You can undoubtedly add to this list. And all of us can celebrate that we are blessed to serve and be loved by a Lord whose unlimited power is bound by His goodness and love.

94 | GOD'S 24/7 GOODNESS AND LOVE

It is good to give thanks to the Lord,
And to sing praises to Your name, O Most High;
To declare Your lovingkindness in the morning,
And Your faithfulness every night,
On an instrument of ten strings,
On the lute,
And on the harp,
With harmonious sound.
For You, Lord, have made me glad through Your work;
I will triumph in the works of Your hands.

PSALM 92:1-4

Have you discovered the truth that the psalmist proclaimed in today's opening verse? Do you know from experience the good that results when you give thanks to the Lord and praise Him?

When we spend time thanking God and praising Him, our problems seem to fade, even shrink. Maybe the reason is as simple as we are no longer focused on them. Instead, our gaze has been lifted higher, and we are looking heavenward to our incomparable, sovereign God. When we think more about His power and goodness than about our weakness and sin, we can remember His faithfulness with gratitude. In trust we can ask Him for guidance, wisdom, peace, and hope.

Spending this time with the Lord enables us to approach the day with a sharper awareness of His presence. And having a lighter heart because of it means living with joy and being able to love others with His love. Such sweet communion with the Lord also prompts the important question, "Why don't I make it a practice to declare His loving-kindness in the morning, to celebrate His faithfulness at night, and to enjoy His company every minute in between?"

95 | WHO PRAYS FOR YOU?

The Spirit also helps in our weaknesses. For we do not know what we should pray for as we ought, but the Spirit Himself makes intercession for us with groanings which cannot be uttered. Now He who searches the hearts knows what the mind of the Spirit is, because He makes intercession for the saints according to the will of God.

ROMANS 8:26-27

Life in this fallen world, populated by sinful, selfish human beings like you and me, can be overwhelming. We all encounter disappointment and loss. We hurt people and people hurt us. Bills, medical diagnoses, job layoffs, ailing parents and needy kids, loneliness, a lack of purpose, and many other circumstances can leave us at a loss about how to pray. We may persist for a while, but soon we find ourselves merely going through the motions, and our prayers may dwindle to nothing.

Look again at today's passage and the hope-filled news it offers. When we don't know how to pray or when we're feeling exhausted, discouraged, or hopeless, the Holy Spirit Himself "makes intercession for us." He prays for us "with groanings which cannot be uttered," a statement that implies heartfelt love for us and a profound desire for God to work in us, in our circumstances, in the hearts and lives of people we care about, and in complex current events across the country and around the world.

What a marvelous ally to have when we encounter life's demands, struggles, and losses! We could ask for no better Helper. God Himself—God the Spirit—prays with divine wisdom and love. He is our Intercessor as well as our Comforter during our pilgrimage on this earth.

96 | WHEN YOU WALK THROUGH THE FIRE

"Fear not, for I have redeemed you;
I have called you by your name;
You are Mine.
When you pass through the waters, I will be with you;
And through the rivers, they shall not overflow you.
When you walk through the fire, you shall not be burned,
Nor shall the flame scorch you.
For I am the LORD your God,
The Holy One of Israel, your Savior."

ISAIAH 43:1-3

When the fires and storms of life strike, we may find ourselves doubting God's love for us. Why would He allow these circumstances—and why does He seem so far away when we clearly need Him?

We love and serve—and we are loved by—a God whose thoughts are beyond our human understanding, and His ways can be very different from what we think we want or would have ever asked for (Isaiah 55:8–9). Of course we want a God who is far wiser than we are, but we often find ourselves pushing that truth aside when we encounter the pain and struggles of life.

Let's consider the comfort and hope of Isaiah's words:

- "Fear not" reveals God's knowledge of our circumstances and our hearts.
- Being called by our names is relational and bonding.
- "You are Mine" speaks to our deepest desire to belong.
- "I will be with you" is a promise that changes not the circumstances but us. We can find comfort, peace, and hope in God's presence.
- "I am the Lord your God" reminds us that we are loved by the all-powerful ruler of all creation and all history, yet at the same time He is our God.

Life's very real fires and storms prove less daunting when we keep our eyes on our God.

97 | "SEE THE SALVATION OF THE LORD"

I know that the LORD saves His anointed;
He will answer him from His holy heaven
With the saving strength of His right hand.

Some trust in chariots, and some in horses;
But we will remember the name of the LORD our God.
They have bowed down and fallen;
But we have risen and stand upright.

PSALM 20:6-8

In David's day, chariots and horses meant prestige, power, and protection as well as dominance over lesser enemies. Having chariots and horses gave people reason to expect victory in battle, but while they wouldn't offer any real protection in modern warfare, they weren't invincible in David's time either.

Remember when, according to God's command and under Moses' leadership, the people of Israel left Egypt? Finally they would be free, no longer slaves. Yet before they were even out of the country, Pharaoh's army came after them on horses and chariots. The people were terrified and angry that Moses had positioned them between the sea and the Egyptian soldiers. Then they heard their leader say, "Do not be afraid. Stand still, and see the salvation of the LORD" (Exodus 14:13).

God enabled His people to cross the sea on dry land. When the Egyptian army followed, God no longer held back the waters. The sea swept over "the chariots, the horsemen, and all the army of Pharaoh . . . Not so much as one of them remained" (v. 28).

The Lord will save you just as He saved His people from the Egyptians. Put your trust in the One who never changes. He is the same almighty deliverer today that He was for Moses and His people Israel.

98 | FINDING STRENGTH FOR TODAY

Then he remembered the days of old,
Moses and his people, saying:
"Where is He who brought them up out of the sea
With the shepherd of His flock?
Where is He who put His Holy Spirit within them,
Who led them by the right hand of Moses,
With His glorious arm,
Dividing the water before them
To make for Himself an everlasting name,
Who led them through the deep,
As a horse in the wilderness,
That they might not stumble?"

ISAIAH 63:11-13

Today's passage offers a good reminder for those times when we are struggling and wondering where God is. And we all have times like that.

When Israel faced God's righteous anger—much like when we are struggling through pain-filled days—they "remembered the days of old." The people's exodus from slavery in Egypt was understandably the high point of God's great provision and protection. The plagues ravaging their captors, the angel of death passing over Jewish homes, the guiding cloud by day and pillar of fire by night, walking across the sea on dry ground, seeing the waters come together and decimating the Egyptian army—great is God's faithfulness. In the same way, thinking back can strengthen us in the present.

So, take some time right now to remember "the lovingkindnesses of the Lord" and His "great goodness" toward you (v. 7). In fact, write down every blessing you think of. Just as we are more aware of red lights than green lights, we can easily become blind to or forgetful of God's goodness to us. Then—again, because we, too, easily forget—consider sharing your list with a longtime friend who, having done life with you for a while, will undoubtedly remember at least a few instances of God's faithfulness that you don't.

99 | GOD'S GRACE AND MERCY

We ourselves were also once foolish, disobedient, deceived, serving various lusts and pleasures, living in malice and envy, hateful and hating one another. But when the kindness and the love of God our Savior toward man appeared, not by works of righteousness which we have done, but according to His mercy He saved us . . . that having been justified by His grace we should become heirs according to the hope of eternal life.

TITUS 3:3-5, 7

Our salvation is God's gift of grace and mercy to us. Grace can be thought of as our getting what we don't deserve, specifically, God's loving pursuit of us, His forgiveness, His faithfulness, and His enabling us to recognize the truth about Jesus.

In contrast, mercy means we *don't* get what we *do* deserve. Look again at the very descriptive first sentence in today's reading. Such sinful behaviors deserve punishment and merit separation from a holy God, but "according to His mercy [God] saved us." In the ultimate act of mercy, God didn't pour out His wrath on us, which we deserved. Instead, He offered the grace of His salvation.

And if that isn't remarkable enough, we didn't have to do anything to earn that gift of salvation. Paul's statement is quite clear: "Not by works of righteousness which we have done, but according to His mercy He saved us."

In what we think, say, and do, we fall short of God's standards and deserve His wrath. But when we recognize that we miss His mark and we confess those sins, we receive salvation instead. We did nothing—and we couldn't have done anything—to earn that forgiveness, righteousness, and adoption into God's family. That's the gospel!

100 | RESPONDING WITH LOVE

Make a joyful shout to the Lord, all you lands!
Serve the Lord with gladness;
Come before His presence with singing.
Know that the Lord, He is God;
It is He who has made us, and not we ourselves;
We are His people and the sheep of His pasture.

Enter into His gates with thanksgiving,
And into His courts with praise.
Be thankful to Him, and bless His name.
For the Lord is good;
His mercy is everlasting,
And His truth endures to all generations.

PSALM 100:1-5

Throughout the pages of this book we have looked at incredible statements about and evidence of God's love—evidence both concrete (His incredible creation, our resurrected Lord's victory over sin and death) and intangible (the gifts of peace, joy, and hope in Him that we can know no matter what is going on in our lives and in the world).

We've also acknowledged what an appropriate response to God's love looks like. Most important, we are to love God with all that we are, and we are to love our neighbors as ourselves, treating them the way we want to be treated. We've also considered some of the choices we have—choices to trust, serve, worship, and surrender; to be joyful, prayerful, obedient, and faithful.

Psalm 100 offers a beautiful summary of God's love for us as well as examples of how we can respond to His love with our love. The psalm includes praise that God welcomes us into His presence, created us, claims us as His people, and shepherds us. The psalm also celebrates God's goodness, mercy, and enduring truth. May we respond with the psalmist's joy, glad service, singing, reverence, humility, thanksgiving, and praise.

Great is our Lord and greatly to be praised!

NOTES

1. *Strong's Concordance*, s.v. "baar," Bible Hub, accessed May 21, 2024, https://biblehub.com/hebrew/1198.htm.
2. *Merriam-Webster*, s.v. "righteous (adj.)," accessed May 21, 2024, https://www.merriam-webster.com/dictionary/righteous.
3. C. S. Lewis, *Mere Christianity* (New York: Simon & Schuster, 1996), 116.
4. *Merriam-Webster*, s.v. "hypocrisy (*n.*)," accessed April 19, 2024, https://www.merriam-webster.com/dictionary/hypocrisy.
5. *Middle English Dictionary*, s.v. "hap (*n.*)," accessed April 19, 2024, https://quod.lib.umich.edu/m/middle-english-dictionary.
6. Brother Lawrence, *The Practice of the Presence of God: And the Spiritual Maxims* (Mineola, NY: Dover Publications, 2023), 79.

ABOUT THE AUTHOR

Jack Countryman is the founder of JCountryman gift books, a division of Thomas Nelson, and is a recipient of the Evangelical Christian Publishers Association's Kip Jordan Lifetime Achievement Award. Over the past thirty years, he has developed bestselling gift books such as *God's Promises for Your Every Need*, *God's Promises for Men*, *God's Promises for Women*, *God Listens*, and *The Red Letter Words of Jesus*. Countryman's books have sold more than twenty-seven million units. His graduation books alone have sold nearly two million units.

DISCOVER PRAYERS AND SCRIPTURE TO GUIDE YOU THROUGH ANY SEASON OF LIFE

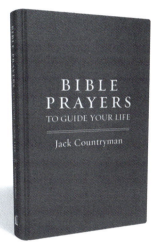

ISBN 978-1-4002-4183-5

This book of topically organized scripture offers prayers straight from the Bible that will equip you with the tools you need to guide your life each day. With scripture on topics such as prayer promises, preparation for prayer, and attitude and conditions for prayer, you will find what God's Word reveals about prayer.

FIND CALM IN THE CHAOS

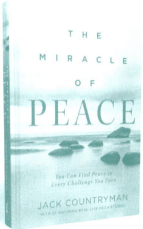

ISBN: 978-1-4002-3552-0

God has instructed us in the Bible not to worry about tomorrow. It sounds simple, so why is it so difficult to find peace? Explore what the Bible says about letting go of anxiety and fear and embracing a new way of thinking that brings you into a closer relationship with God.

Available at bookstores everywhere!

LET GOD DRAW YOU NEAR

World headlines and our personal struggles can leave us feeling weary and anxious. But life's questions and our emotions are not new to God. If you are feeling exhausted, worried, or lonely or are facing difficulties, *The Power of Hope* by Jack Countryman offers a beautiful reminder that the same God who comforted and blessed the people of the Bible can offer you transformation and peace today.

ISBN 978-1-4002-2496-8

Available at bookstores everywhere!